The Practice of History in India

Essays in Search of a New Past

Anirudh Deshpande

The Practice of History in India: Essays in Search of a New Past
Anirudh Deshpande

First Published 2020

ISBN 978-93-5002-680-9 (Hb)

Published by
AAKAR BOOKS
28 E Pocket IV, Mayur Vihar Phase I
Delhi 110 091 India
aakarbooks@gmail.com

Laser Typeset at
Sakshi Computers, Delhi

Printed at
Sapra Brothers, Noida

It is a strange paradox that the historian, who is concerned professionally with the past, plays a crucial role in the future of the society which he is studying. The historian's interest lies in trying to understand the emergence and the evolution of a society in a historical perspective, where the term society includes every aspect of a people's life. As a result of his investigations, the historian creates a picture of the society. In his handling of the evidence from the past, he is often influenced by his own contemporary setting. Historical interpretation can therefore become a two-way process–where, the needs of the present are read into the past, and where the image of the past is sought to be imposed upon the present. The image of the past is the historian's contribution to the future.

–Romila Thapar in *The Past And Prejudice.*

Contents

Preface

The main object of teaching is not to give explanations, but to knock at the doors of the mind...Those who pin their faith on university examinations as the test of education take no account of this.

–Rabindranath Tagore in *My Reminiscences.*[1]

Every book and all written, spoken or visual history has a purpose and, more often than not, this purpose is political. There is really nothing called knowing the past for its own sake. When people say they are curious about the past they must ask themselves the reason for their curiosity. The process of knowing history begins with an ontology of the self. That is so because all curiosity emanates from a social and political context within which the seeker of information is located. Therefore, the questions and answers of history do not exist outside a systemic context. The social identity of everyone and their relationship with the omnipresent power in social relations are central to this context. That is why the history of class, caste, religion and gender is important. Obviously a Brahmin or Rajput views history differently from a Bhil or Mahar. There are many social identities we often assume unselfconsciously; the job of history is to encourage the self-interrogation of these identities. This self-interrogation leads us to

1. *Omnibus*, Vol. 2, Rupa, New Delhi, 2003, p. 467.

the problematic of power. Knowingly or unknowingly the existence of humans is governed by their relationship with power and one of the most important tasks of history is the investigation of this relationship. The origins, evolution, change and permanence of economic, social and political power comprise the stock of human history. Undergraduate students of history are often not conscious of this relationship because of the false consciousness inculcated in their minds by society and its conformist schooling system. To many of them history remains a chronicle of battles and dynasties. The education they receive in schools is designed to convert them into larger or smaller cogs of the system. This is what 'career counselling' from Class 7 is all about. Schooling in most bourgeois systems is neither designed not executed with the aim of creating a rational, conscious and sensitive human being appreciative of reasoning and social justice. Many students end up doing history because the system has rejected them. It is a different matter that most of them thank their stars at the end of our courses. Once their interest in the subject is aroused and they connect with it personally there is no stopping them. There are numerous stories of social rejects who become fine writers, teachers, film actors, film makers after learning critical history inside or outside the university. It is not surprising that the greatest writers always evince a deep understanding of history without necessarily being professional historians. Who can deny that there is much history to be learnt from the works of Balzac, Hugo, Dostoyevsky, Tolstoy, Tagore, Premchand, Gorky, Lu Shun, Faulkner, Marquez, Allende and Llosa among many others.

This book is meant for students of Indian history and its related subjects. It is also underpinned by the assumption that teachers, like me, remain lifelong students of history. My research students, friends and colleagues in the colleges of Delhi University are aware and appreciative of my modest contributions to the craft they share with me. It has been a long standing demand of these good people that a book like this should flow from my pen.

This book is about the practice of history in India or better still my preferred idea of the historian's craft, the history of which is coterminous with human civilization. The obvious question quickly arises. There are so many books on doing history so why should another one be written and also published? The answer to this question may be sought in my vocation as a practising historian who has always keenly felt that a book like this ought to be written for the graduate and postgraduate students in India. School students are also welcome to read it as are those people who read history in general.

The doors and windows of historiography are open to everyone.

Since 2005 I have taught history in Delhi University, a public funded university, to students who flock to it year after year in the hope of a better future. The majority of these students come from socially and economically deprived families. Many of them cannot speak or write academic English. They understand simple English but are usually overawed by the formidable language in which a large number of ivory tower academics write. Numerous public school educated English-speaking students also join Delhi University every year. Their problem is different. They are uncomfortable with Indian languages and often ignorant of rural and small town life. We teach history in a country where the north does not know the south and the east does not know the west. Teaching Indian students is a great learning experience. I have learnt a lot of history while responding to the questions of my students who comprise a heterogeneous social group. The method I have followed in my classes and outside them has been bilingual and dialogical. I have never approached my classroom with the banking concept of education so beautifully criticized by Paulo Freire in *The Pedagogy of the Oppressed*.

This book may be read as a condensed report of my conversation with history since I developed an interest in history as a school and university student. I have used snatches of this conversation in my classes in the course on the schools and methods of history taught to the MA First Semester students in Delhi University. The chapters of this book are expanded versions of the various aspects of this conversation which has taken place between history *and* me and also between my students, friends and family members *and* me. It does not pretend to be an exhaustive reader or primer on the *historian's craft*. There is no jargon on method and methodology in this book. Readers who want to read books more comprehensive than this one should consult the works of R.G. Collingwood, E.H. Carr, Marc Bloch, C. Wright Mills, Jean Chesneaux, Paul Thompson, Romila Thapar, Richard Evans and John Tosh. I particularly recommend *The Pursuit of History: Aims, Methods and New Directions in the Study of History*, Sixth Edition (Routledge) by John Tosh to my students and friends. A list of readings has been provided at the end of this book. I was not inclined to burden the readers with an exhaustive bibliography in the age of Wikipedia and Google Search. Some of the books mentioned above contain good bibliographies in any case. Readers can choose books and articles from them in accordance with their historical interests.

This book has seven chapters.

Chapter one underlines the difference between literature and history. Unlike fiction which emerges from the largely imagined individual and collective memories, professional history is based on primary and secondary sources which verify the historian's truth. History seeks to narrate the truth or at least the probable truth on the basis of facts. Compared with literature, written history shares an uneasy relationship with memory because of its institutionalized modernization since the 19th century. The chapter asserts the need to expand the horizons of history by approaching memory more constructively than Indian historians usually do. Doing this in India means reckoning with the memory of the vast majority of Indians excluded from the petty-bourgeois academic construction of knowledge. Several modes of remembering the past have flourished in the pre-literate, literate and post-literate contexts of Indian society since the early 20th century outside the enclosure of professional history. It is suggested that written history and unwritten memory must both be used critically and dialectically by the historian. The historian can begin by interrogating his vocation to examine why history, once a popular discipline, has declined in pedagogical importance since 1947 in India. Since 1947 the popularity of the audio-visual media has increased manifold while the significance of class-room history has witnessed a serious decline despite the expansion of the post-colonial Indian education system. Thus we have reached a globalized condition in which myths masquerade as history in the media to the detriment of the historians' profession and social harmony alike. This calls for a greater intervention of the historians in the media in the interest of a responsible and critical public history. In sum, historians must consciously write and teach histories sensitive to the contemporary times. The good news is that modern historiography has constantly evolved since the 18th century not as an esoteric discipline but as a politically relevant subject.

Chapter two raises the issue of oral history, a much debated method of doing contemporary history among historians. It says that modern oral history, as a sub-discipline of history, probably began as a method of recording the experiences of people during the Great Depression in the United States. Before that the survivors of the Civil War had been interviewed by scholars. After 1945 "the interviewing of eye witness participants in the events of the past" developed steadily as a history genre of recording individual and collective memories. Begun as an initiative to record the popular memories of war, this method became full-fledged oral history over time. Oral history is related to, but different from, oral tradition which, according to the late Jan Vansina's definition, must be at least two generations old. The future of oral history is predicated on the fact that professional and institutionalized histories are deficient in recording the histories 'from the inside' of the oppressed. Oral history is an aid to the movements for social justice across the world. It is particularly significant to countries like India where literacy is low and the memories of the oppressed are routinely erased from public memory. The chapter demolishes the difference between the oral and written and questions the assumed superiority of the written in mainstream historiography. It presents a critique of establishment historiography and suggests that historians adopt a receptive and balanced approach towards several forms of remembering the past. Oral history reorients the historian's craft in interesting ways. It is crucial to the histories which flourish outside the dominant narratives of modern societies. The fact that cross examined testimony was central to history writing since the times of Herodotus has been forgotten by the professional historian obsessed with the archive of written and published documents.

Chapter three attempts a similar exercise with reference to what we can call the visual archive. The visual archive presents embodied human memory on a wide canvas spread over time and space. In time it extends from the cave paintings to the age of photographs and film. Since the 19th century the visual archive available to historians has become huge and must be taken as seriously as the documentary evidence provided by the past. The inherent ability of the visual to challenge or support the documentary accounts of the past has to be appreciated by the historian in search of holistic history. For instance, the histories of art, architecture, photos and films have increasingly informed written histories in myriad ways for a long time. Photos and films often undermine heavily subjective histories. Both Chapters two and three also say that in practising oral and visual history the historians should not get carried away by their material. Issues of criticality and corroboration maintain their salience to the craft despite the political leanings of a historian. The connections between the local, regional and continental which underpin oral and visual evidence should always be given priority in analysis by the oral and visual historians.

Chapter four raises the issue of paying attention to imagination in the conception and writing of history. Almost all historians agree that good history can only be written with the aid of imagination and this makes history a cousin of literature. In 1984 when I appeared for the JNU MA entrance examination, one of the questions, I remember, asked: What is the role of imagination in the writing of history? Whether history is considered an art like the late medievalists and Renaissance writers thought while writing *Ars Historica* or a science like in the modern times, only an imaginative historian can write learned prose and, thereby, history that is both meaningful and enjoyable. Historical fiction is the bridge between history and fiction in the same as the economy is a bridge between society and geography. Like the writers of prose learn from history, historians learn from fiction. For many people historical fiction is the window to serious academic history. People interested in stories of the past read literature set in a historical context and this fertilizes their imagination. The interaction of fiction and history is usually not explored or taught in history departments though departments teaching cinema history touch upon this subject. Taking a novel of the late Kiran Nagarkar set in medieval Mewar as its focal point, the chapter explores the exciting possibilities of researching the cultures of our ancestors highlighted by good historical fiction.

Chapter five lengthens the line of thought laid down by Chapter four by delving into military history and its portrayal in cinema. We must note that the internet archive of war films and documentaries is massive. Since the beginning of photography and cinematography war has been a favourite of photographers and filmmakers. Why and how is war filmed? What lies behind Bollywood's nationalist obsession with war and the armed forces? These questions are answered in the chapter which is based on the assumption that mainstream Bollywood commercial cinema is basically a socio-cultural discourse of the bourgeois nation state in India which leaves little room for dissent.

Chapter six is a commentary on B.R. Ambedkar's historical method, an important subject usually neglected by Indian history departments. In the 19th century the Dalit-Bahujan perspective on Indian history and caste relations was developed by the critical works of Jyotiba Phule and the *Satyashodhak Samaj* (1873). Savitribai Phule was the head of the women's section of this truth seekers' society. At the same time nationalist history writing dominated by the Brahmins and other upper caste men developed in the Bombay and Bengal Presidencies. In most Indian history departments, the historical works of men like R.G. Bhandarkar and M.G. Ranade and others are taught. Students are made aware of the emergence of a new crop of Indian historians from the universities established in India by the British in the 19th century. Rare is the department which takes the works of Phule, and their fruition in Ambedkar's writings, seriously. Even the Indian Marxist professors who champion the cause of the oppressed usually do not pay adequate attention to this important subversive school of historiography. The chapter seeks to redress this imbalance by illuminating the fact that Ambedkar was not only a leader of the depressed classes, lawyer and constitutional expert par excellence but also a critical historian who truly wrote history 'from below'. His research method of deconstructing texts and reliance on logic and cross examination of sources is a salutary example to all aspiring young Indian historians.

The last chapter of this book raises the question of the individual in history. One question all students of history have been asked since time immemorial is: What is the role of the individual in history? The question has elicited a variety of answers which may or may not support the 'great man' theory of history. Usually the query is framed in a patriarchal context and therefore the word individual in it refers to a male. A female here or there may enter the ranks of such individuals but usually she does so by acting like a politically 'great man.' Indira Gandhi, to take only one example, is remembered best for the defeat of Pakistan and creation of Bangladesh in 1971 by a country obsessed with masculine national pride. The chapter asserts that while it is important for historians to assess the role of specific individuals in their historical context, it is equally important to know why and how some men are presented to us as 'great'. What is the process by which the story of kings, queens, politicians, diplomats, generals and so on becomes legendary in history? The chapter refers to the concept of layered memory to understand the mystique of 'great men'. The ruler chosen is Chatrapati Shivaji Maharaj who is central to the modern Indian imagination of the Mughal period, especially the reign of the last great Mughal Emperor Aurangzeb.

This preface will be incomplete without a word of thanks I owe to a number of men and women for enriching my life and travels in history. Students and colleagues have always been helpful in numerous ways and to name everyone here is impossible. I am especially indebted to my wife Anupama Satyal and sister Anjali Deshpande. Both these women are my best critics. Anand Kumar, my brother-in-law, has always heard and appreciated what I say and in a deeply personal way my route to Ambedkar has been guided by his presence in our lives. Shefali and Urvashi never hesitate to remind me that I am also a father besides being a historian. Discussing things with them over a spicy mutton curry has often cleared my mind. My friends Milinda Wakankar, Yasser Arafat, Shraddha Kumbhojkar, Babasaheb Hariba Dudbhate, Umesh Bagade, Dev Kumar Vasudevan, Amar Farooqui, Prabhu Mohapatra and Vikas Gupta have been kind enough to discuss a lot of history with me over the years and some traces of these discussions have naturally found their way into this book. Such gratitude is felt, not described in words. Parul Pandya Dhar deserves a special word of thanks for reading a draft of this Preface. Her comments have been addressed. I am indebted to Nayanjot Lahiri, former colleague and now Professor of History at Ashoka University, who read and commented on the first unpublished draft of the essay on oral history many years ago. My former and current research students Manoj Sharma, Sandeep Chatterjee, Muphid Mujawar, Saurabh Vatsa and Shakir Hussain deserve a jumbo sized thank you. They are not only capable historians in their right but also my friends and confidants. From their engagement with social issues I learn a lot of history. K.K. Saxena of Aakar Books has dealt with the manuscript with great efficiency. I thank him for promptly agreeing with my proposal and publishing the book in an easily readable format.

The usual disclaimer applies.

1

The Balance of History and Memory

> When I was a student, we were ordinarily taught as scientific historians to peel away the fictive elements in our documents so we could get at the real facts.
>
> –Natalie Zemon Davis[1]

Introduction

Some years ago the scholars Partha Chatterjee and Jan Breman expressed the optimistic view that Indian social science research was "more engaged with social reality than its counterpart in the global North."[2] As an historian of modest standing I would like to suggest that this generalization may apply to Indian sociology, social anthropology or feminist and labour studies but is certainly not true of Indian history as a discipline per se. In fact, we would be happy to see a flourishing of a socially engaged public history in India away from the myths peddled as history on social media or in books written by ideologically mischievous individuals. Compared with the involvement of professional historians in the making of public history in the West, Indian historians fare poorly. The reasons why I find myself only in partial agreement with the scholars mentioned above comprise the subject of this chapter.

As historians, or aspiring historians, let us start with the basic problems our vocation faces in India today. In general, becoming a historian in the democratic republic of India is a risky proposition. The studying of history beyond the highlighted sections in your school textbooks blights your job prospects. Career counsellors, in their paid tutorials, in no Indian school advise their wards to become historians. In general, they discourage students from pursuing a teaching career for reasons well known to my readers. Thus only those who are exceptionally courageous, different or unable to become doctors, engineers or business executives opt for history as a graduation subject. Having done so they realize that in India everyone is a historian. History is not a preferred discipline in Indian schools and universities but every Indian is at least a weekend historian on social media. While history was never a first choice of students in pre-globalization India its status declined steeply after 1991. In any case, globalization promotes amnesia about capitalism and therefore history as a discipline has suffered terribly at the hands of the 'market forces' since 1991. I remember being laughed at by the upwardly mobile in the early 1990s as a history doctoral student in JNU. There is another serious problem the historians face in India because for all its democratic pretensions modern India does not have a civil society in the British sense of the term. The great filmmaker Satyajit Ray once called the Indian audiences backward and the same can be said of most Indian readers. I have used Britain as an example because it is said that we learnt modern democracy from them. Let us not forget that the Constitution of India is largely based on the Government of India Act 1935. Matters on this democratic score were always complicated and have become worse since 2014. In India doing history can easily get you into serious trouble with the state. Your stated or unstated political inclinations or the narrative of your book may easily make you a target of the bosses who control the mobs maddened by identity politics. For writing about a historical or even mythical character who may or may not have existed five hundred years after the end of the Neolithic period can land you in jail, or for better or worse, in a hospital or morgue. In the light of these probabilities I think many readers will congratulate themselves for the guidance they gave to their children after reading this.

Of all the humanities in India, a word I prefer to the cage like 'social sciences', perhaps the position of history is the most ironical. Unknowingly every Indian seems to have taken the late Eric Hobsbawm's adage that *everyone is a historian* seriously. All Indians are doctors and historians in media, buses, trains and airplanes. Indians flaunt, and often contest, their heritage without gathering a sound knowledge of the subject. They trust their tourist guides and WhatsApp forwards but do not want their sons and daughters to become historians because at the end of the day only money pays and while history has nuisance value it has little money in it. The past is a crucial component of the cultural nationalism to which Indians are addicted, but history, as a rigorous discipline, is not to their liking. Most Indians do not like mixing culture and history because their understanding of both is generally ahistorical. It is safe to assume in such laboured circumstances that unless a tolerance for varied history becomes ingrained in Indian society the community of Indian historians might as well be doomed to eventual irrelevance. History and its sister disciplines have in any case been allotted a small role in the blue print of a 'knowledge society' for India conceived by its technocratic planners in the recent past. Hence a large part of the historians' problem may be located in the fact that the market and the sciences have dominated the national imagination in India since 1991 and this has helped marginalize the humanities in Indian education further. A large part of the problem can also be seen in the way Indian historians treat their own vocation. The third part can be seen in the discomfort history causes to quotidian politics in India because history is a continuous battle between the social need to remember the past and the political imperative to make society forget or distort it. Let us be frank: we live in a post truth society in which the learning of scientific history comprises a relatively minor role in the education of the masses addicted to social media and WhatsApp forwards. In the life of millions, as the critical journalist Ravish Kumar of NDTV has often repeated, the university has been replaced by the WhatsApp university. In time if the public university is privatized into self-financing institutions which will cater to the affluent the importance of history as a taught graduate or post graduate subject will decline further. It will continue to be taught in the private universities as part of liberal arts or humanities but only a select few in society will afford a degree in it. I cannot imagine Indian parents paying a few lakhs for a college degree in history when the same amount can be spent on vocational subjects or sciences which give students greater employment opportunities.

So much for the institutional problems faced by the discipline of history in India. Let us now put on board some observations on memory, the starting point of history for most people. History means to remember the past in connection with the present and future and professional history means to recount the past scientifically and systematically. Memory is important to history but it is not history in the same way as the root is important to the tree but should not be confused with the fruit. Memory may pass as the subjective understanding of one past by an individual or group of individuals but whether such subjectivity can be called history is a difficult question to answer. A peasant, tribal, worker, professional or woman remembers history as a local experience in general. This locality of history is significant to the writing of popular history but unless this locality is contextualized in regional and world history the subject of history remains partially forged and the subaltern realization of history remains incomplete. Thus it is suffice to say that a contextualized, systematized and rationalized understanding of memory comprises history and to remember this means remembering the difference between fiction and history. The relationship between fiction and history is the same as that between imagination and being. In this context literature is better placed to deal with memory because it is not bound by the academic compulsions of academic history. If nothing works, literature can even call upon 'magic realism' to serve its purpose but history cannot do so. For many school students, like me, historical fiction is an important gateway to history.

Compared with literature modern history's relationship with memory is complicated. Literature and memory sit together comfortably because the former has the universal right to take liberties with the latter. In contrast the historian's relationship with memory calls forth a method, or craft to use Marc Bloch's word, which a litterateur may dismiss with a condescending smile. Ancient and medieval historians, as historians, almost always made copious use of memory in writing their chronicles. For later historians the works of these historians became the 'primary' sources of history to be used with discretion and in corroboration with other sources. Historians writing ancient history commonly, and confidently, have always used the epics and other such memory-based sources rationally in the practice of their craft. Thus individual or collective memory dealt with critically became an integral part of written history. As Marc Bloch noticed, Europeans first heard that the sun both rose and set over the oceans from memories transmitted to travellers by the sailors whose accounts were used by Herodotus the so-called father of historiography. Such observations were present in the literature produced by seafaring long before the geo-centrism of the medieval world was overthrown by Copernicus. Yet this information, a constructed narrative of facts like written documents, could not overthrow the Christian orthodoxy prevalent in Europe for many centuries[3]. This proves that memories of objective phenomena can lie hidden under layers of hegemonic culture for centuries. Memory, arguably, can often be as credible as written narratives which became the fetish of positivist history in 19th century Europe. In sum, whatever the source–oral, written or visual–the historians' method, which endows the sources with meaning within a theoretical framework, remains central to their understanding of the past[4]. Whether you agree with the submissions of a historian is a different matter. In that case your opposition to the fellow should be based on a superior interpretation of sources. It cannot, and should not, emanate from prejudice and rhetoric as is normally the case.

This essay analyses the methodological and other problems arising from the need to expand the horizons of history by means of constructively returning to the visual expression of memory in a post-literate context[5]. In India this could well translate into looking at visual narratives in a state of pre-literacy for the majority of people thanks to our education system or the lack of it. People, in general, remain outside the field of dominant history. Social marginality and its popular memory, which is often captured in several still and motion pictures, are central to the process of everyday living in India. For instance, a contemporary history of popular distress during the 2016 demonitization or Covid-19 pandemic of 2020 cannot be written without reference to the huge visual evidence generated by both events. Similarly, to observe another example, no research thesis on events such as the Bhopal Gas Tragedy of 1984 or communal riots in India can even begin without a reference to the visual and oral evidence created by such tragic moments of Indian history. Compared with professional history a variety of visual and oral memories have flourished in the pre-literate, literate and post-literate contexts of Indian society since the early twentieth century. Their close relationship with constructions of social and political memories, and thereby the entire conception of popular history, is undeniable. And yet at least till the 1990s oral and visual history was neither taken nor promoted seriously in most Indian history departments. In Indian schools, private and public both, history has been reduced to a small portion of the social sciences. From Class 11 when it is taught, the truncated syllabus is geared to rote learning and exams. Many middle class students have good smart cell phones which they use for non-academic purposes but rare is the history teacher who inspires them to put this splendid technology at the service of critical knowledge including a history of their fellow compatriots.

History learning has been reduced to textbooks and boredom. The spaces vacated by the retreat of good history have been filled in by an irresponsible media. Fake news thus depends on fake history but this book demonstrates that this need not be the case.

We concentrate on this issue from the perspective of historians searching for new kinds of histories with the help of more 'peopled' sources in contrast to the traditional precepts of history writing which privilege official documents over other forms of evidence. History, cinema, television and the oral domain together make sense of the past and there is nothing wrong if all of them are made to collaborate in the simultaneous writing and making of history. By taking both the academic and non-academic approaches to the past as constituent, and not necessarily opposing, parts of his subject the historian stands to profit. Further, the historian needs to carefully analyse the history of his own vocation to see why and how has history, as a taught subject, gradually lost a great deal of its popularity over time. There is nothing wrong in interrogating knowledge and schooling itself and there is much to be gained by interviewing your neighbours and workers and photographing your surroundings to witness historical change first hand. In Indian schools a subject called Socially Useful Productive Work (SUPW) was introduced some decades ago by a state desirous of cultivating social empathy among high school students. This involves 'social work' outside the school. Students who have not much idea of social empathy till they are fourteen or fifteen are suddenly supposed to learn a thing or two about their society. If empathy is cultivated by the media of oral and visual interviews among school students right from Class 6 or 7 the SUPW would make more sense. Why can interactions with peasants and workers not be made a part of practical school learning right from an early age? After all, what is education supposed to achieve beside the creation of bourgeois individuals dedicated to the pursuit of careers and money?

With an eye on the necessity of forging the subject of history appropriate to current Indian conditions this submission is divided into four parts. Part one comprises a brief survey of the changing trends in modern historiography. Part two is a description of the process of making, un-making and re-making of history in the modern world. Its aim is to establish the resilience of history as a viable practice of the humanities. Part three identifies the causes of the problems faced by historians and professional history in our times. Part four offers a few suggestions which might help regenerate history as a discipline in India with reference to the dynamism in historiography visible elsewhere. A critical engagement with the media in all its forms can help Indian historians widen their social perspective and deepen their cultural insights. This might prove momentous in revolutionizing the Indian historians' craft in future. We must note that Indian historiography has usually developed in response to periodic developments in historiography in Britain, Europe, North America and the former colonies. This response is often combined with the new historical discourses demanded by Indian society over time. This modest voyage on the vast ocean of historiography is predicated upon the hope that Indian historiography, despite official apathy and hostility, has the capability of self-regeneration. But that can happen only if Indian historians realize that they are part of, and the solution to, the problem of history writing in India. Unless Indian historians effectively reach out to their countrymen, most of whom imbibe their historical sensibility through the oral transmission of knowledge, memory, cinema, television and the internet the future of history as a professional discipline in India looks uncertain. The argument for the historian's intervention in an informed 'public history' remains strong.

I

The historian must be "impartial" in an "honest submission to the truth" declared Marc Bloch in the Bible of historians *The Historian's Craft*.[6] This telling comment comes from a historian who railed against the 'positivism' of Ranke in formulating the basis of the Annales School of history writing in France. And yet, this crucial assumption of modern historiography forces us to reconsider our craft afresh: can the historian narrate the truth? The philosophical problem of truth becoming entwined with historical narrative would not, and indeed does not, arise if history is perceived as merely one of the several subjective interpretations of society developed by intellectuals. The main tenets of post-modernism rest on exaggerating the subjective nature of description. According to the post-modernist or his ancestor the phenomenologist the existence of history itself is an impossibility because all observation is deeply subjective. But since Bloch, Carr or someone like Richard Evans would not subscribe to post-modernism the question of approaching the truth in the past remains with us. Logically speaking if truth does not exist in the past it cannot exist in the present and cannot, therefore, exist per se at all. If all past and, thereby, present is fiction life itself is fiction and all knowledge is speculation. The problem with the post-modern condition is that it exists in a material modern world where institutions sustain it. These institutions themselves are historical and not mythological. To criticize modernity is one thing but to say that all modernity is contrived, and thereby, of no use to humanity is quite another. What will a post-modernist professor do if his department clerk does not make his pay cheque in the subjective belief that he does not work in the department? Obviously the learned professor will produce proof of his having taken classes in the department to claim his salary. And what is that salary? Where does it come from? Is it part of the social surplus generated by the country's production process? So, in the end, material history matters. Let us leave post-modernism for a while and turn to historiography.

To begin with, we ask why and how did modern historiography arrive at the possibility of narrating the truth about the past? Before the emergence of institutionalized professional historiography, narrating historical experience was an exercise in the reproduction of the past through the modes and social agencies of collective representation. The task of remembering the past and transmitting it over generations was handled by the traditional intellectuals of pre-modern societies for a long time before the emergence of modern historiography. In all unequal societies–tribal, slave, feudal and bourgeois–history has always comprised an ideologically contested terrain. The origins of history lie in pre-historic cave paintings and the memory based epics which were developed over generations before being committed to paper in their numerous community specific versions. Right from the beginning remembering the past was enmeshed with the communitarian imaginative sensibilities closely tied to group identity and politics. Hence, since the earliest times, historians, both traditional and modern, have shared an intimate relationship with both orally transmitted and written memories in order to weave their narratives in the context of class/community/national contests. Thus history, quite like literature, is essentially the art of narrating the past in as interesting and meaningful a manner as possible although historians generally assume that since they narrate the truth they are different from the composers of fiction including historical fiction. However, unlike literature, a product of the plunder of individual and social memory, modern professional history is based on certain defined, and periodically redefined, 'sources' which verify the historian's generalizations. Thus the reference to credible evidence is said to mark the difference between history and literature. Further, since the historian's narrative is always located in a contested ideological context, history is forever open to challenges posed to its existing state by historians and non-historians alike. Examples of such challenges abound. For instance, Karl Marx and Frederick Engels attacked specialized political, diplomatic and military history even as these were being consolidated as history in the European university departments during the 19th century. The original Marxist accounts of the revolutions in 19th century Germany and France and the class struggle in Reformation and post-Reformation Germany were written from a perspective truly critical of the extant event and personality-based bourgeois notions of history[7].

Critical history arose alongside professional seminar-based history.

But Marx was not alone in digging below the events and their enticing descriptions by the academic intellectuals of his day with the help of a new critical rhetoric of proletarian class struggle. The romantic 'popular' historians of the 19th century, like Jules Michelet for instance, marginalized political, military and diplomatic history in search of a popular social and cultural history based on a reinterpretation of historical sources including folklore. By the end of the 19th century, the founders of the Annales School, who stressed the role of geography, economy and historical sociology in the writing of history, began moving in directions which overhauled the historian's craft[8]. At the same time the German historian Max Weber was pioneering a historical perspective to which a study of comparative sociology, religion and social psychology was central; what Marx did with the political economy of capitalism, Weber achieved with reference to the cultural superstructure of capitalism. The decades before the Second World War witnessed the flowering of the *Annales* and Marxist schools in Europe despite the similarities and differences between them. The Marxists, in particular, gained strength because of the rising working class movements in the latter half of the 19th century in France and Germany, the Bolshevik Revolution, the popular reactions to Fascism and Nazism and the Spanish Civil War. In addition to Marxist historiography the working class movements also gave rise to the anarchist perspective–a forerunner of latter day post-structuralism. Following the Second World War while Marxist and Nationalist historiographies gained prominence in most former colonies, in France and Europe historiography witnessed a significant shift towards a post-structural paradigm developed by scholars like Michel Foucault. This tendency was also expressed in the works of intellectuals like Edward Said who equated colonial historiography with the Orientalist project scripted by colonial scholars and administrators primarily to subjugate and rule the colonized. Foucault deconstructed the *epistemes* of historiography which had dominated modern Europe since the Enlightenment and implicated history and the historian in a scheme of knowledge and power created by modernity. By arguing that history is never independent of the historian's language, ideology and culture Foucault, a historian of medieval and early modern Europe himself, dealt empiricist history a blow from which it never recovered[9]. This revolution in history writing, which emerged from both within and outside the discipline of history, has been relentless in its quest for a new, significant and more meaningful narratives of the past.

Foucault and Said developed a powerful critique of linear bourgeois progressive history. Both scholars, like the Italian Marxist Antonio Gramsci, criticized the intellectual assumptions of modern history writing. The idea that the historian was not implicated or could not be implicated in his project of history writing had emerged in the 19th century. This idea was demolished by these three scholars who were historians themselves. After these people the historian could no longer write history without a sense of self-interrogation. History writing became a self-reflective exercise and went beyond the vantage point narratives developed by historians like Macaulay in the 19th century. But self-interrogation has its limits. With the rise of post-modernism philosophical self-reflection became intellectual self-doubt. Gradually a set of historians emerged whose sole preoccupation with history was 'deconstruction.' To these historians, paradoxically, history appeared to have become in the hands of historians themselves a carefully constructed mythology validated by footnotes. And we finally arrived at the "poetic act" hypothesis of history writing promoted by Hayden White. More on this below.

Matters reached a stage where post-modern theorists like Keith Jenkins wrote of bidding goodbye to history and living without "histories of either a modernist or a post-modernist kind"[10]. Thus post-modernism shifted from a world of modern narratives to the academics of "endlessly open narratives" before rejecting history altogether[11]. The post-modern turn is an epistemological break from the revolution in historiography described above and has influenced emerging trends of 'doing' history without the help of established historical methods. An important consequence of post-modern thinking, besides the prevalent tide of anti-Marxism among historians in general, is the re-establishment of an empiricist 'subjective realism' in the works of some historians who assert that nothing exists outside the text. A denunciation of all constructed history, irrespective of political differences between historians or the variety within Marxist historiography, has also been expressed by some scholars who are particularly harsh on the Marxists[12]. Following the publication of Hayden White's critique of history in 1973, the chorus against treating professional history as a viable discipline grew louder in certain academic circles on the basis of de-linking the future from the past during the last thirty or forty years[13]. In sum, the post-modernists criticize history for being a subjective narrative imposed on selected facts by historians by the use of linguistic devices. In the post-modernist submission, since all historical narratives are poetic acts performed by historians, it is impossible to access a verifiable objective past through the historian's carefully constructed imaginary plot of events. Hence, and logically following the post-modern submission, all history is subjective history and therefore there is not much to choose between several carefully constructed interpretations of the past. The positivist construction and Marxist reconstruction of the past, are therefore, unreliable narratives. If history is thus reduced to a project of cultural relativism and ideological subjectivism it becomes easy to first denounce and later reject it altogether. According to White, the acknowledged guru of Jenkins, all narrative history is exactly the opposite of the claims made by historians in its defense. In this scheme of things there is no difference between 'verifiable' history and 'unverifiable' myth–the past, simply put, cannot be known and what cannot be known is of no use to knowledge. The problem of the pay cheque, alluded to earlier, remains important nonetheless.

According to White the "rules set up by professional historians for the licensing and vetting of historians–unlike those set up in chemistry or physics–are purely conventional and their authority purely customary. History is a practice utterly lacking in the theoretical foundations normally required for the establishment of a practice as a modern science"[14]. But is this assertion true? Does science not evolve by a dialectic of the inductive and deductive methods? Let us place White in context. It may be true that White debunks traditional history writing in general his original argument must be understood as a critique of 19th century history which appealed to the raw facts venerated by statists like Leopold von Ranke and his followers. Since the positivist method, according to which scientific history based on documentary evidence reveals the truth, tends to colour general modernist history the post-modernists apply White's concept of 'Metahistory' to virtually all emplotments of history available to the modern reader. The critics of White can refer to slavery or industry or patriarchy to ask whether histories of these comprise myths? Are Lincoln and the Civil War mere creations of historians? Hence to distinguish between good and bad history or true and false history is quite different from the logical culmination of post-modern thinking. Since history is politically and ideologically used by the agencies of nationalism, state and capitalism its essential political nature cannot be ignored by the historian.

The critics of the post-modern position blame White and his followers for encouraging and legitimizing historical revisionism and obfuscating the crucial political difference between fact and fiction[15]. They have often asked for clarifications from the post-modernists on issues such as the Holocaust, slavery or the treatment of native Americans by the European colonizers in America. The politics of the post-modern remains problematic because history has not always been written in the way in which it has been conceived by the post-modernist. Contrary to the position held by Jenkins and his guru, Coleman believes that historians committed to the politics of social justice can produce 'demonstrably credible constructions". Zagorin, after criticizing Derrida's *Of Grammatology* as the "canonical formulation" of the post-structural and post-modern philosophy, dismisses post-modernism, like Kant would have in the pursuit of practical–as opposed to pure–reason, by concluding that scepticism "is not a dwelling place for the human mind."[16] Bloch has dealt with this perennial problem in his work. He once met a man who disbelieved everything which was written and fell for every rumour he heard! That is the result of hyper scepticism. Confronted with the huge amount of evidence presented by history the post-modernist must retreat.

In sum, historians learn a lot from the post-modernists but when the post-modernist starts demolishing all forms of knowing, and thereby knowledge itself, the historian can turn around and ask a few legitimate questions. If no one can know, how can the post-modernist know? And if the postmodernist does not know better why should the modernists, including the majority of historians, take him or her seriously? Why is the post-modernist implicated in the institutionalization of knowledge through the university system? What exactly are the politics of the post-modernists except a pathological dislike of Marxism promoted by a Western academic establishment actively developed by Cold War politicians? After all the deconstruction of a narrative, a linguistic device mastered by the post-modern scholar, invariably generates a counter-narrative. Since the thesis is always present in the antithesis the post-modernist counter-narrative must be subjected to the same rules of criticism which are applied to the first narrative[17]. If the historian's history is based on his political choice, the post-modernist's disdain of history serves his institutionalized practices. The assumption that post-modernism is, or even can be, apolitical is the height of naivete. In our view post-modernism is as constructive as traditional or Marxist or Feminist or Black or Working Class or Tribal or Dalit histories despite its intellectual pretensions.

II

The flourishing of history in numerous Western universities suggests that history seems to have got the better of the post-modernist challenge. Since history is deeply embroiled in power, it is always affected by social and cultural change. Its writing expresses power struggles in society in the same way as the conception of knowledge in general. Therefore, the struggle between subversive memory and curated public opinion is central to the politics of both hegemony and history. Unfortunately, the relation between conditioned memory and hegemony is overlooked by the academic historian in search of an 'objective' history. The best place to forget this relation, ironically, is the modern temple of history writing: the official archive. The story of modern historiography, a chapter of modern history itself, is interesting and informative. It dates back to the European Enlightenment of the 18th century which was first dominated, and later hijacked by the hegemonic ideologies of industrial capitalism. By the beginning of the 19th century written history became the handmaiden of the European bourgeoisie in Europe and the masters of the new colonies. The work of James Mill and Thomas Macaulay, to quote two well known examples in the case of both Britain and India, is an outstanding example of bourgeois scholarship. Leopold von Ranke, the historian honoured by the Prussian state, converted history into primarily political history in the latter half of the 19th century. In doing so he gave a conceptual form to the trends anticipated in the historical writings which had already become fashionable in European literate circles in the first half of the 19th century. While the growth of a culture informed by the spread of printing and the rise of personal libraries, debating clubs and scholarly journals contributed its bit to the discourse of civilization among the educated Europeans, the development of the universities in the 19th century removed history from the community to the lecture room. History became a dominant European and North American perspective when Western Europe and the USA became, in the words of Gabriel Garcia Marquez's Nobel Speech, the "two great masters of the world." Guided by these masters and written by their agents in the servile colonies history came down to the colonial subjects as a story which did not belong to them. It was a history from "above" and far which was intended to make the colonized feel inferior.

The construction of history as a project of the universities, set in motion by bourgeois modernity, was nourished by nationalism in all modern nation-states and their colonies following the American and French Revolutions and the Napoleonic Wars. Following Europe, nations were imagined as repositories of histories everywhere. Thus the colonized mind was corrupted for centuries. Since the early 19th century, the colonial-national binary became the dominant paradigm of history in schools and colleges the world over. Nations emerged even where the basic conditions of nationality were absent. History became a history of the nation–either established or dominant or aspiring to arrive on the international stage and the European aspirations thus became world aspirations with tragic post-colonial consequences. This nation could be ancient, medieval, modern, barbaric, cultural, linguistic, religious or racial in varying contexts. Historical voices which threatened the dominant narrative of the nation had to be suppressed and, if possible, silenced altogether. Since the late 18th century the national paradigm has dominated history almost in all modern nation states but it has failed to erase historical memories which give rise to periodic rebellions in historiography. Wherever the nation marched, it created the 'other' and thereby the need for alternative history.

The construction and deconstruction of history developed simultaneously much before post-modernism arose as a challenge to scientific knowledge. The social contradictions within the capitalist societies and between colonialism and the colonies were noticed in great measure by scholars in the 19th century. Enlightenment, besides the discourse of civilization and nation, also produced the tools by which the ideology of capital and nation could be challenged. On the one hand it produced liberalism and on the other Anarchism and Marxism. History, and historiography, became a contested narrative of hegemony or counter-hegemony depending on who wrote it. While political history was being consolidated within the framework of the nation-state in the universities and establishments across Europe, history, as subject and ideology, was critiqued by intellectual-activists like Marx and Engels outside the realm of academic history.

In criticizing the claims of capitalist modernity the Marxists, in our view, became the first scientific post-modernists. Marx's belief that true human history lay in mankind's liberation from and transcendence of the capitalist mode of production was the most revolutionary philosophy born in the conditions of modernity in the 19th century. Marx was not a professional historian but he gave history a revolutionary economic, structural and class content by inserting into it concepts such as the forces and relations of production and surplus value. Further, on questions of property and issues such as the urban housing problem, Engels carefully deconstructed the available research on the subjects. He also wrote one of the first inspiring histories of the English working class from the Marxist perspective which remains a classic till date. Political, diplomatic, military and elite history was also attacked by cultural and popular historians like Jacob Burckhardt, Jules Michelet and some American historians in the 19th century. These historians were the pioneers of popular history and laid down the foundations of the Annales 'revolution' which ultimately resulted from a synthesis of economics, geography, sociology and psychology. Thus, almost all the ideas expressed in the 20th century 'history from below' can be traced to the work of the revolutionary and romantic intellectuals of the 19th century–a century of capitalist expansion, defeated proletarian revolutions and rising working class trade union movements. The 19th century was momentous for other reasons. The Spanish Empire in America unravelled in it. The American Civil War which ended in the abolition of slavery in the USA happened in the middle of the century. The women's movement began with the suffragist agitations and there were massive popular rebellions against foreign rule in several parts of the world including India and China. These produced narratives which challenged the presumptions of statist academic histories of the period.

It is a different matter that the founders of the *Annales* approach, probably because of French national pride and the unworthy example set by Stalin, were hostile to Marxism. Nonetheless the Annales pioneers were deeply influenced by the prominent socialists of the day like Juarez who had written a monumental history of the French Revolution which inspired Lucien Febvre. Some of the Annalists survived the German occupation during the Second World War and became influential within the French history establishment during the post-war decades. Marxism had never lost its academic salience among an influential and large section of the French and British historians kept reasserting itself as a critique of the past and present establishments. For instance, Jean Chesneaux's *The Past and its Future–Or What is History For?* (1976), published soon after the American defeat in Vietnam, and in the context of the worldwide anti-imperialist student movement of the late 1960s and early 1970s took the establishment French historians to task for their collusion with Eurocentric and imperialist history[18]. In this terse volume, Chesneaux drew upon his vast knowledge of China, Japan and Vietnam to inveigh against the imposition of academic distance, chronology, quadri-partition, temporality and Eurocentrism on world history by European historians of the establishment. Chesneaux's aim was to bridge the intellectual gap between the practitioners of professional history and their popular subjects by making the power politics of history writing and teaching transparent. In the 1970s mainstream establishment history was also criticized by the Feminists. Such criticisms also included a Marxist history *sans* structural determinism exemplified best in the work of E.P. Thompson who stressed the volition of the working classes in his classic *The Making of the English Working Class.* Feminist history and workshop history, which gathered strength in the context of the Vietnam War and the 1968 student rebellion in the US and Europe, comprised other important attacks on elitist establishment history. The Occupy Wall Street and Black Lives Matter movements of our times are worthy successors of those attacks. The 1970s, 1980s and 1990s also heralded new genres of cinema which created critical narratives no historian could ignore. For instance, the typical Second World War films gradually gave way to a disturbing and realistic portrayal of modern warfare. More of this is discussed in a separate chapter in this volume.

The way in which historiography has reinvented itself from the early 19th century till the present demonstrates the potential of history as an interdisciplinary subject. In each challenging political moment of world history historiography was enriched by a new creative interaction with politics, economics, geography, sociology, anthropology and science. Its large source list, which was periodically revised, comprised archaeology, memory, official and non-official documents and folklore. Later on photography, radio, cinema and television became crucial sources and expressions of history. Since the American Civil War and the Crimean War all written history was incomplete without photographs. Despite the long-standing reservations of professional historians regarding these new sources of history rebellion persisted. Only now is it overcoming the historian's orthodoxy. In this context we must remember what the American filmmaker D.W. Griffith predicted in the early 20th century. In future, he said, children would be "taught practically everything in moving pictures" and, therefore, would "never be obliged to read history again."[19] Fortunately or unfortunately, we find ourselves living in that future although children are still obliged to read several histories to which they cannot relate. Today the media, including the internet, is important to the historian and his students for the following reasons. One, it is indispensable as a source and manifestation of contemporary ideas and culture. Two, the historian can influence public opinion by using the media. Three, the absence of official transparency can often be made up by a meaningful and committed media as shown by the Wikileaks project. This gives the historian a new, and more critical, perspective on the official sources and the print media. Four, several history sites place a variety of primary sources within easy grasp of historians who wish to use the internet to write history. Five, almost all history organizations, including the oral history associations of many countries, place their material on their sites. To put it differently–we look at the media in the same way in which Michelet cast his eyes on popular literature in the 19th century; popular history today is impossible without the media. Ruth Balint puts this across succinctly:

> The public, and indeed many students of history, receive far more historical information from the media than from the pens of historians. Historians might prefer to read books, but when it comes to history, the general public prefers to watch television[20].

III

The discipline of history has declined in India because of the practices of the establishment of Indian historians and the emergence of a cultural milieu favourable to technology, management and the market in modern India[21]. The portents of this unfortunate occurrence were visible decades ago when Nehru put India on the road to scientific and technological progress. Hence the decline of history in India should be located in a national context which has generally been unfriendly to the humanities despite the fact that Nehru was an accomplished historian. It is a fact that the general quality of undergraduate and postgraduate students who opt for history, because they cannot qualify for more lucrative courses, has declined since 1947. Further, the teaching of history does not inspire academic confidence in the country. Rarely do we meet a school student who likes history these days. Given this sorry state of affairs, the time has come to examine how Indian professional historians are at least partly responsible for the decline of their subject. My experience confirms that the condition of History, like Hindi, is so bad that students with the lowest percentages end up opting for these subjects. Such is the malaise afflicting a subject which has produced India's most acclaimed scholars since the colonial period. Ironically the great majority of Indian historians have done precious little to save and revitalize their discipline in keeping with the changing demands of time. History, except in a small circle of central universities and research centres, remains a prisoner of positivism in the vast majority of India's demoralized, under-funded and substandard, colleges and universities.

Indian historians express concern about the decline of their vocation as a matter of routine but their annual Indian History Congress, the world's largest organization of historians, entertains a flood of papers the great majority of which might not get published ever in an academic journal. For many reasons the great majority of Indian historians have not been trained to handle the crisis of their subject. Only a handful of them engage seriously with their students and the media. In the absence of systemic support, their responses to the predicament can range from the tragic to the comic. Some would like history to be converted into an 'applied' vocational subject like tourism and historians into tourist guides. Others try their best by offering less commonplace solutions by borrowing concepts and courses uncritically from syllabi taught in the Western universities. Most of the regional universities are happy teaching basic courses designed decades ago; new courses imply new readings which are disliked by teachers and best avoided by the majority of students who depend on the notes supplied to them by their seniors and the photocopy stalls near their departments. The spirit of adventure, which may still linger in certain places, is blighted by the forces of linguistic, caste, religious and regional chauvinism in most places. The icing on the cake has been provided by the recruitment of teachers by the selection committees comprising senior professors. The policy of selecting college teachers in India, in general, is based on patron-client relationships and has entrenched mediocrity, sycophancy and complacence to the detriment of students and subject alike. It is well known that the material and intellectual conditions in the Indian regional universities is bad–the politics of caste, religion, region and language govern the recruitment of teachers and the teaching of history there. Financial corruption in faculty and staff recruitment is not unheard of. However, the seriousness of these problems on one hand should not occlude the dynamism of Indian historiography, an irony of sorts, on the other.

Professional history developed in India under colonial tutelage during the 19th century. It was coloured by colonial ideology and indebted to Whiggish methods and perspectives. Central to Indian historiography, especially from the last quarter of the 19th century, were facts, events and individuals as they were conceived by the Whig historians of Britain. Colonial accounts of Indian history were challenged in India by the nationalist historians who used the tools of historiography imported into India by the British. But it must not be forgotten that the imagination and narrative of a nation, either through its denial or assertion, was central to both these schools of historians. The Indian nationalist historian, above all, was a representative of the Indian middle class looking for a nation in Indian history which vindicated his anti-colonialism. Marxism also began to emerge as an important and revolutionary force in Indian history writing after the First World War because of the Bolshevik Revolution and the growing international popularity of communism in the 1920s. Nonetheless, despite its several noteworthy achievements, it could not completely overthrow the nationalist paradigm which dominated the Indian schools and universities after 1947; during the colonial years in their criticism of capitalist colonialism and imperialism the Marxists were the fellow travellers of the nationalists despite significant differences between the two. Later, as the Marxists entered the university system of India during the 1960s and 70s, some of them lost the edge of their scholarship and became establishment Marxists in the same way as some of India's communist parties became 'official' parties integrated into the bourgeois-democratic apparatus of the Indian state. The official Marxist scholars were deeply influenced by the social democracy of India's official left whose Marxism found a safe sanctuary in the institutions patronized by the Indian state. Since the 1990s the nature of the Indian state has changed. It has become visibly right wing and majoritarian. The history it patronizes was born as communal prejudice in the 1920s when the Hindu nationalist RSS was established with the dream of a Hindu Rashtra.

In the 1980s, the Subaltern Studies project, inspired by the works of Antonio Gramsci and the development of Marxist humanism in European historiography since the late 1960s, emerged as a revolt against the elitism of official Marxism which had steadily travelled a great distance from a true people's history of India since the colonial times. On the other hand, several assumptions of the Indian nationalist and Marxist historiography were undermined by the 'revisionists' inspired by the so-called Cambridge school. Unfortunately, and despite the promise they held out to enthusiastic young scholars, the Subaltern Studies and the revisionist projects have ended up becoming esoteric enterprises. Their influence remains limited to a small section of metropolitan India and some Western universities which have active South Asia departments although it must be noted in passing that the revisionists, by their thorough empirical researches, have contributed immensely to our understanding of several medieval and early modern Indian regions. In the 1980s the mainstream nationalist and Marxist histories in India were also seriously challenged by the rising labour, feminist, Dalit, regional and cinema histories and the partition narratives. All these histories started using, and simultaneously constructing, oral and visual archives quite impressively in their redefinition of caste, community, sexuality and the nation to challenge the dominant paradigms of Indian history. Some Indian historians who wanted to develop the inter-disciplinary potential of history, and who also probably wanted to distance themselves from the nationalists and the Marxists, looked towards the Annales perspective for inspiration in the 1980s. It is a different matter that when this happened the Annales had lost much of its thematic coherence and some Marxists had risen to prominence within its ranks. Historiography is in a flux in contemporary India and yet a lot needs to be done to revive popular interest in it. The following section suggests ways in which this can be achieved.

IV

The audio-visual media is a space which historians can use to counter myths and popularize a history based on reason and a critical reading of the sources. But this is easier said than done. India has a large, well established and influential film industry which is central to the self-perception of millions of contemporary Indians. India also has among the largest TV audiences today; rare is an Indian who reads in bed these days. The Indian audio-visual media employ scores of writers, photographers, directors, area 'experts' and hundreds of thousands of blue-collared workers and artists on a daily basis. For an average Indian the media is both a source of entertainment and upward mobility. The internet, cinema and television comprise the chief source of information and entertainment for the majority of Indians. Even marriages are arranged on the net these days. Property and other commercial transactions take place regularly on the net. Further, the audio-visual media in India is enmeshed with the advertisement and retail industry both financially and ideologically. This complex ideological super-structure is imposed over a Third World country which, if things do not change post-Covid-19, might become the first Fourth World country in the world. The numerically small 'great Indian middle class' with its motorcycles, cars, condominiums, public schools, malls, call centres and an abundant supply of cheap labour dominates Indian print and audio-visual media. This media, within which much of perceived Indian history is reported, developed gradually in the last sixty years without attracting adequate attention from Indian historians.

Compared with the media whose dynamism grows daily, most of professionally written history about India after 1947 is hobbled by the lack of 'primary sources.' Government rules, which forbid the release of classified documents to the archives, place severe restrictions on historians who wish to write a well-rounded history of contemporary India. Faced with such problems it is only natural to expect Indian historians to expand their source base in search of new histories but, in general, this has not happened. The condition of oral history is worse. Unlike the USA, Britain, Australia and Malaysia, where rigorous oral history is integral to critical popular history, India has no oral history association. There are a few oral history archives in India and one of them is tucked away in the Nehru Memorial Museum and Library in New Delhi and that too is not popular in orientation. Research students, almost as an iron rule, are ordered by their supervisors to examine archival sources to begin their dissertations.

In contrast, and given the regressive method pioneered by Marc Bloch, students can easily start their work with interviews and other forms of social observation before moving on to documentary evidence. But the historians' obsession with the official archive blocks this line of thinking. For example, if a young historian were to write a history of the Operation Blue Star of 1984 or the Gujarat and Delhi riots of 2002 and 2020 with the help of official sources he would not go very far. However, if work is begun with a methodical approach to an oral history of these corporate and communal crimes and then expands to the large corpus of available unofficial sources, a first class dissertation would materialize in a matter of months. In the India of today even that might be difficult if not altogether risky to do. The importance of oral history or media history in an urbanizing country like India cannot be underestimated at the school, college and university levels. Although the belief that cinema or media 'studies' offers the students an easy option compared with rigorous archival work is on the decline, resistance persists.

The engagement of historians with films, by which we mean all films, has yielded a method of analysing them despite the ideological differences between film scholars. At the moment, as Toplin points out, film historians borrow "overarching concepts" from Freudian, Marxist, feminist, post-modernist and deconstructionist perspectives, it may be added, in the same way as other historians. In comparison there are others who, being "uncomfortable with the jargon or the ideological perspectives of the theorists", follow an eclectic path[22]. No matter how we approach the problem it should be remembered that visual narratives have always been 'read' as documents by experts and the public alike. The method of treating film as a source of history has been developed by historians like Marcia Landy and Pierre Sorlin. The second part of the method, following the submissions of film historians like Robert Rosenstone, consists of treating film as an independent narrative. Both submissions are based on the understanding that "an analysis of motion pictures and television programmes can yield insights into the conscious and subconscious concerns of people in another time and place much as a study of literature can produce insights."[23] In the accumulated material of film historians films and television appear as a "cultural product" to the historian; an important source of history. Following the insights provided by the cultural materialism of Raymond Williams, it should be understood that the study of the making of a film is as important to the historian as the form and content of the film itself. The path ahead is mentioned by Toplin in the following words because the arising of a general enthusiasm for a historical study of films is merely the beginning of a journey:

> Now that the study of film has won a degree of respect in the profession, it is appropriate to ask which techniques of analysis need further development? Which questions about film and history deserve greater attention? How can historians working with film bring a greater degree of sophistication to

their craft? Indeed, how can they prod each other, demanding that studies of the moving image break new ground and deliver new insights to scholars, students and the public?

The experienced film historian, and a founder of the *Film & History–An Interdisciplinary Journal of Film and Television*, John E. O'Connor mentions the four ways indispensable to a historian's understanding of film. The first is to see film as a representation of history. The second is to view it as a medium providing an insight into past cultural and political values. The third is to scrutinize it as a kind of historical evidence; to 'read' it as a conventional document. The fourth is to carry out a study of the film and television industry in order to examine the context from within which the visual narratives emerge. Toplin adds an important dimension to these four by emphasizing the popularity of a film as an important field for the historian. Why do certain films flop while others succeed at the box office, therefore, could be important to analysing a film historically. The differing class appeal of a film is equally important to film history. Toplin also stresses the importance of television history to modern societies in which people generally spend their entire evenings watching TV programmes. Since the messages of TV "compete aggressively" with or, it may be added, reinforce "society's traditional influences on youth," historians should take TV as seriously as cinema. Finally, Toplin highlights the importance which historians must attach to actively associating with the process of filmmaking. Examples prove that with some training and self-education historians can become amateur filmmakers with the aid of affordable easy-to-use technologies available in the market[21]. The critical combination of oral, visual and documentary evidence provides the historian a great opportunity to intervene in and possibly change public history and many levels.

Conclusion

This essay has examined the evolution of modern historiography and identified the challenges which history, as a discipline, faces in India. It has also focused attention on the limitations imposed upon historiography by the elite professional historians who are not entirely blameless when we discuss the decline of history as a subject. We have underscored the difference between the social decline and social relevance of history. However, in disagreement with the post-modernist assertions dealt with above and the claims of the votaries of globalization, we believe that the time to say goodbye to history, and thereby the historians by implication, has not yet arrived and, in all likelihood, will not arrive in future. Critics of history forget that the past, present and future of society are related in a way which makes history relevant forever. Even if the market completely dominates society in future, history will retain its importance. Markets require histories of justification and hence, *inter alia*, promote business history or myths favourable to their claims. In contrast, opponents of the market will provide correctives to the dominant narratives by raking up memories from the debris of civil society. The continued existence of an unjust society based on profit, class, caste, race and patriarchy highlights the need to study history because of its abiding ideological importance. The history of society will remain a history of an ideological contest despite the end of ideology proclaimed by the votaries of globalization in the 1990s. It is true that a serious decline of history in Indian schools, colleges and universities has occurred because of several reasons which the historians cannot address on their own.

But Indian historians can rise to the occasion by changing their habits and making their narratives more interesting and widely accessible. To do so, their choice of topics and methods must undergo a radical transformation in sync with changing historical conditions. Above all, history must become meaningful to the students whose eyes, unlike those of their esteemed professors, stay firmly fixed on the future. To achieve this, Indian historians can negotiate a new path to the means by which the great majority of Indians connect with history in their daily lives. The audio-visual media and oral history provide a heterogeneous source of inquiry and opinion to our students. A lot of history is seen, heard, felt, debated, accepted and rejected by our students in this variegated field and sites like the WikiLeaks and Youtube, to name only a few, have changed our view of the internet. Many documentary and visual archives are available on the net. The historical sociology of the Indian media has an interesting story which began with the remarkable socio-psychological thesis of the pioneer Panna Shah published in 1950[25]. Since then, and following the submissions of scholars like Laura Mulvey in the 1970s, a number of media historians have developed a corpus of inspiring work for both teachers and students[26]. Since the 1970s the popular perception of history has changed.

Indian historians have periodically expanded their horizons since the colonial times in response to changes in historiography abroad and the demands of Indian society. Time and again their vocation has taught them that in wrestling with their predicament they have nothing to lose but their habits. Now, once again, the time has come for them to focus attention on the media and oral history to rejuvenate their subject, and particularly the histories of the marginal groups, like their predecessors did in the 19th and 20th centuries. It would be in their interest to treat contemporary India as a vast and varied oral and visual archive. To begin with, there is a lot to learn from the active Oral History Associations [OHA] in several countries and the access to information made possible by acts such as the RTI Act. Scholars like P. Sainath, for instance, regularly use the information collected by the RTI activists to write critical historical articles located in the present. The several OHAs have accumulated a large mass of material and expertise since the late 1940s when oral history was launched as an integral branch of popular history. Indian historians can access this material and adapt the methods developed by the OHAs to Indian conditions. Despondent friends, whose mood can easily be understood by the critics of globalization, often tell me that they cannot do much about the threat posed to history by the market. While this dejection is understandable it will not help matters because the tendency to wait for the inevitable, and practise what is familiar in the meantime, is too well entrenched within the establishment of Indian historians. Predictably much will not change soon. Nonetheless, if Indian historians peruse the evolution of their subject they will come to the conclusion that the market, including the media, is both a threat and an opportunity. In the ultimate analysis a lot depends on how the historians link the market, the media and non-professional kinds of histories present in society to write and project on screen histories relevant to the future based on "pluralistic approaches."[27] The historian in contemporary India should not forget that he lives in the time of WhatsApp forwards and fake history peddled by paid trolls. He faces a strong well-funded organized alliance between popular history and communal ideology which makes his task of writing and disseminating critical history quite difficult. The choice is clearly between crafting good public history on media and leaving the field to the trolls bent upon destroying civil society. Since history, as a discipline, has overcome the most serious ideological challenges posed to it during the 1970s and 80s the time has come for historians to assert themselves more confidently than ever in the public domain.

NOTES

1. *Fiction in the Archives Pardon Tales and Their Tellers in Sixteenth Century France.* Stanford: Stanford University Press, 1987, p. 3.
2. Ravi Srivastava, 'Social Science Research in India in a Medium-term Perspective', in *Economic and Political Weekly*, March 17, 2012, p. 20.
3. *The Historian's Craft.* New York: Vintage Books, 1953: Indian edition, Delhi: Aakar Books, 2017, p. 80.
4. The importance of method to all kinds of history writing is emphasized in Simon Gunn and Lucy Faire (eds.), *Research Methods for History.* 2012. Edinburgh: Edinburgh University Press.
5. In a post-literate context many people can but do not read as a matter of choice.
6. *The Historian's Craft.* p. 138.
7. Some outstanding Marxist historical works comprise *Manifesto of the Communist Party*, *The Class Struggles in France*, *The Civil*

War in France, Revolution and Counter-Revolution in Germany, The Eighteenth Brumaire of Louis Bonaparte and *The Peasant War in Germany*.

8. For details see Peter Burke, *The French Historical Revolution: The Annales School 1929-89*. Stanford: Stanford University Press, 1990.
9. An interesting discussion on Foucault's attack on positivist history is present in Alun Munslow, *Deconstructing History*. London: Routledge, 1997, (Special Indian Edition, 2007), pp. 129-148.
10. *At the Limits of History: Essays on Theory and Practice*. London: Routledge, 2009.
11. Ibid., p. 14, defines post-modernism "as a general term under which lived (and live) varieties of post-structuralism, post-Marxism, post-feminism, post-colonialism and deconstructive currents, etc."
12. See Munslow, *Deconstructing History* in general.
13. Hayden White, *Metahistory: The Historical Imagination in Nineteenth Century Europe*. Baltimore: John Hopkins University Press.
14. 1973. In this work White laid down the basis of the post-modern scepticism regarding history by asserting that because history writing is a "poetic act", involving a deep seated emplotment of themes, historical objectivity is a myth cultivated by the tribe of historians.
15. Willie Thompson, *Postmodernism and History*, Palgrave Macmillan, New York, 2004. Also see Perez Zagorin, 'History, the Referent and Narrative–Reflections on Postmodernism Now' [Originally published in *History and Theory*, 38, 1, 1999]; Rejoinder to a Postmodernist [Originally published in *History and Theory*, 39, 2, 2000] and Michael C. Coleman, 'Response to a Postmodernist: Or, A Historian's Critique of Postmodernist Critiques of History' [Originally published in *American Studies in Scandinavia*, 34, 1, 2002]. The articles by Zagorin and Coleman have been reproduced by Jenkins in the *At the Limits of History* along with his responses to the forceful defence of history provided by these two scholars. A balanced assessment

of White can be found in Paul Sutermeister, *Hayden White, History as Narrative: A Constructive Approach to Historiography*, December 2004, Scholarly Essay, GRIN Verlag fur akademische Texte, http/www.grin.com (Graduate Institute of International Studies, Geneva (2005).

16. *At The Limits of History*, pp. 120; 75; 83.
17. Patrick Finney, 'Hayden White and the Tragedy of International History', www.allacademic.com (International Studies Association, San Francisco, March 29, 2008), tells us that the post-modernist description of history as "verbal fictions, the contents of which are as much invented as found" forces us to reconsider history as a "repressive ideological project...inimical to utopian thinking" which is crucial to construct a better world tomorrow. The force of post-modernism has shifted the attention of history writing to historiography, i.e. an endeavour to know why and how history was written in the past in favour of what happened in history. However the role of the historian is larger than teaching historiography in the same way as that of a doctor who must diagnose illness, prescribe medicines and try his best to cure the patient after telling him how and why particular illnesses were treated a hundred or fifty years ago.
18. I have referred to the English edition of this book by Thames and Hudson (1978).
19. Ruth Balint, 'Where are the Historians?', *Inside Story*. July 30, 2009 [http://inside.org.au/where are the historians/inside story].
20. Ibid.
21. It can also be argued, as Amiya Sen did in response to an earlier draft of this essay, that the collapse of history is related to the decline of the 'liberal' tradition and the emergence of an instrumentalist history written to serve vested interests. In saying this Sen is trying to locate a space between the subjectivities of historical interpretation and the existence of a possible objective history.
22. Robert Brent Toplin, 'The Historian and Film: Challenges Ahead', *American Historical Association, Perspectives* (April, 1996) [Sourced from the internet].
23. Ibid.

24. The historian Uma Chakravarty has successfully done this recently with scant regard for an ordered narrative which historians might mistakenly seek in films.
25. For details see Anirudh Deshpande, *Class Power and Consciousness in Indian Cinema and Television.* New Delhi: Primus Books, 2009.
26. Laura Mulvey, Visual Pleasure and Narrative Cinema, *Screen* 16.3 Autumn (1975) [I have read the widely available internet version of this original feminist article].
27. Ravi Srivastava, op. cit., p. 21, summarizes the ICSSR Conference's [February 6-7, 2012] conclusion on Indian social science research in the following words: "There was some debate on whether, and to what extent, Indian social sciences could be developed on entirely fresh and non-Western paradigms but it was generally accepted that Indian social sciences could be based on pluralistic approaches and encourage independence, tolerance and rigour."

2

The Past, Present and Oral History[1]

> As such oral tradition is not only a raw source. It is a hypothesis, similar to the historian's own interpretation of the past. Therefore oral traditions should be treated as hypotheses, and as the first hypothesis the modern scholar must test before he or she considers others. To consider them first means not to accept them literally, uncritically.
>
> –Jan Vansina[2]

> The sociological imagination enables us to grasp history and biography and the relations between the two within society.
>
> –C. Wright Mills[3]

Historians are divided on the question of oral history. Historians like Paul Thompson are pioneers of oral history and emphasize its importance to working class histories. They also point out the oral content in the written sources to demolish the strict division between the two which guides the detractors of oral history. The other extreme is represented by historians like Arthur Marwick who consider oral history unreliable and therefore useless to history writing. Between these two extremes are most of the historians who have conceded ground to oral history, especially while considering histories of the uneducated and illiterate people. Tribal, peasant and women's histories make copious use of oral testimonies. Nonetheless the bias against oral history persists. For example, the third edition of the *Fifty Key Thinkers on History* by Marnie Hughes-Warrington [Routledge, 2015] does not mention Paul Thompson. It is a different matter that his books *The Voice of the Past* and *The Edwardians* can be considered classics of 20th century historiography. Despite its critics oral history has grown by leaps and bounds since the Second World War and commands academic respect in many countries. The historian John Tosh has given it a fair treatment in *The Pursuit of History*, a much read book on historiography and historical methods. This chapter comprises an essay on the relevance of oral history to India in the light of the issues mentioned above.

Since memory is central to oral history let us begin by defining the relationship between memory and history. What is history? If the task of remembering is central to history it comprises the dialectic of selected individual and collective memories. Historians know that the past is informed by the conflicts of the present and imaginations of the future; connecting the past and future makes history an interesting problematic. Currently, because the oral and written are confounded on social media, the historians' responsibility to their vocation has assumed a new seriousness. Since all narratives and traditions survive at the intersection of the past and present, traditions "must always be understood as reflecting both past and present in a single breath."[4] Divested of this principle, epics and folklore would mean nothing; the variations in the epics and the conflicts they represent signify the conflicts in the societies which produce and reproduce them. Critical history contests dominant ideologies in all historical contexts. In contrast, the false separation of politics and history follows Leopold von Ranke's dictum:

> History has had assigned to it the office of judging the past and of instructing the present for the benefit of the future ages. To such high offices the present work does not presume: it seeks only to show what actually happened [*wie es eigentlich gewesen*][5].

Till the 19th century, when the modern classroom and seminar emerged in the European universities, non-professional historians wrote history. In Europe intellectuals like Bodin, Bacon, Voltaire, Robertson and Gibbon were not history professors. Intellectuals did not exclude oral evidence from their research. Indeed, an archive-based modern historiography was produced by the nation-state only in 19th century Europe[6]. In pre-modern societies the traditional intellectuals were the historians. A traditional scholar would not have considered his vocation a science because history in the pre-modern world was considered an art–in early modern Europe it was called *ars historica*. Further, the difference between history and literature was blurred in the bardic traditions. Paul Thompson demonstrated in 1988 that oral interviews underpinned written history in the 18th, 19th and 20th century despite the pretensions of the specialists. Oral tradition and the cross examination of eye witnesses were important tools of written history in ancient China, Japan and Europe. The emergence of history as a vested interest of the modern historian who works at an imagined distance from society in the 19th century is underscored by Thompson[7]. The reliance on documentary evidence to produce a dissertation gave to the modern historian a 'self-identification' which all method-based science has. The system perfected in Germany was followed everywhere:

> Nor is it accidental that the cradle of this academic professionalism should have been nineteenth-century Germany, where university professors constituted a narrow patrician middle-class group, particularly sharply cut off through their isolation in small provincial towns, political impotence, and the acute hierarchical status-consciousness of Germany, from the realities of political and social life[8].

Thompson's magisterial analysis of oral history forces us to revisit the subject in the Indian context. In India the distinction between *itihaas* or *tarikh* and a simple *kahani* or *mythyaa* was well known and Indian historians have long ceased to agree with the view that ancient Indians were essentially a-historical[9]. India has a rich tradition of history writing based on oral testimony *inter alia*. The pre-colonial Marathi historical texts, the *bakhars*, are concrete examples of this[10]. The perception that pre-colonial Indians had no sense of history is a myth of colonial historiography disproved further by the *tawarikh* tradition in vogue in medieval India[11]. Compared with fiction, history evolved over centuries as a credible story presented with consummate literary skill. Though memory, history and imagination are inseparable history is not the same thing as fiction[12]. Even Edward Said, a great critic of Eurocentric objectivity, trusted history to speak truth to power[13]. Since history is essentially a narrative of the past, it is impossible for it to ignore memory. Moreover, history is a conflict between remembering and forgetting; like personal memory it thrives in a mode of editing. The editing of knowledge inside and outside the archive informs the historian before history is written. Further the language of history is related to the art of story-telling despite the historians' love of facts. Indeed, the process of writing history on the basis of written sources is an act of imagination similar to oral narration. The difference between the oral and written is located primarily in the act of creating a document. Documents, including most committee and commission reports, generalize knowledge on the basis of oral interrogation.

Nonetheless, it is difficult to say what constitutes the historian's primary narrative–the lecture and archival notes not free of imagination or the wisdom obtained from locales outside the university. Ideas creep into lectures, papers and books from the most unlikely of places. The reputation of the historian concerned and common sense would inveigh in favuor of both expertise and imagination. Conversations with colleagues and friends provide ideas which become embedded in the written and yet the political difference between fiction and history is important to combat the subjectivism promoted by the post-modernist reduction of history to fiction[14]. This makes it imperative that a method for oral history be devised to separate reality from myth in the same way as it is done in the case of documentary history[15]. Thanks to scholars like Thompson such a method has evolved in many countries where oral history is taken seriously. In countries where community and neighbourhood histories are encouraged in schools and universities oral and visual history has become quite sophisticated. Unfortunately in the esoteric establishments of the professional historians oral history languishes. An oral historian, in 1998, wrote the following to highlight the bias against oral history in a country where oral history has been successful outside the universities since 1945:

> Few history departments either teach or encourage fieldwork in oral interviewing or oral history. Few departments are willing to accept either the financial or intellectual responsibilities of oral history projects. More telling is the fact that while the collection and editing of manuscripts or personal correspondence has long been considered a legitimate task both for PhD candidates and established scholars, no history department that I know of would grant a doctorate to one of its students in return for the submission of a set of thoroughly documented and well-conducted oral histories, and few historians would receive wide applause for the publication of carefully edited interviews such as is regularly done in other disciplines. In short, what the profession is saying is that oral history is not a respected practice of history[16].

The attention oral history has received from Indian historians can be gauged by the negligible number of papers published on the subject in the Indian journals. In most Indian states, the practice and teaching of history remains affected by nationalism, caste and religious considerations[17]. However, asserting the oral does not mean that any oral account of the past is authentic. While history is "the story we make of the stories we find", we "have no excuse for uncritical usage" of oral testimonies[18]. Francis Bacon, father of the inductive method, advised historians to apply logic and reason to the vast empirical evidence necessary for historiography[19]. The "conversational narrative" produced by an oral history interview is the *sina qua non* of the oral history method[20]. While the archival sources help to produce a written narrative in conversation with the historian, the oral interview recognizes the active and passive role of the oral historian. Unless the oral historian knows the historical context of his subject the history produced by an oral interview remains incomplete. His informed questions comprise a context for the interview. In sum, oral historians must read sociology, psychology and other subjects which influence historical narration.

Oral history destroys the false dichotomy between the oral and written. To begin with, the sources of a historian, the kind of history pursued by him and his politics are related. The evidence contains narratives which appear fictional at first sight. Natalie Zemon Davis has pointed out that these fictional "counter truths" are important to write cultural, social and gender history[21]. The writings of historians, travellers and scholars who wrote their narratives in the ancient and medieval times have achieved an archival authority but their annexation by modern historiography overlooks their oral and visual content. For scholars of ancient and medieval India the travelogues are important sources but the oral content of these is usually not recognized by historians. Although oral testimony is inherent in written sources the fetish for archived documentary sources drives away the historian from acknowledging the enormous weight of the oral in the written sources[22]. The oral traditions of a society are often expressed in the vernacular and the Indian historian dependent exclusively on the classical languages or English may miss this point altogether. Often the class and regional domination of a language pushes certain forms of knowing the past into the languages of local representation and social protest[23]. Dalit and tribal histories, conceived from within Dalit and tribal cultures, are examples of histories silenced by the ruling classes. The narratives of the oppressed survive the onslaught of hegemony by moving into oral domains. Indeed this "value of emotion", jettisoned by the professionalization of history, remained important to the romantic traditions of history writing in 19th century Europe[24]. This became evident in the dramatic style of romantic historians like Jules Michelet. Emotion transcended national history and inhabited social history; histories developed by the New Left and the history-workshop approach post-1945 are examples of this. Oral history was not entirely new when popular history took a radical turn in 1968. During the 1970s, when popular disillusionment with the post-war world and academics became widespread and tape recorders common, oral history emerged as a tool of anti-establishment history. Without the sensitivity brought to economic and working class history by the individual and collective memories of the workers themselves a new working class history would have been impossible. Contemporary histories of African and Asian countries follow the same pattern. The narration of the 1994 state orchestrated massacre of Tutsis by the Hutus in Rwanda by Philip Gourevitch is a good example[25]. The oral and visual have certainly revolutionized doing history in our age. In India the documentaries *Final Solution*, *Ram Ke Naam* and *Muzzafarnagar Baki Hai* demonstrate new ways of conceiving and executing history in the times of communalism and corporate media hegemony.

In the 19th century positivism converted professional history into a rigorous exact national record of the past. This trend has continued despite developments in the humanities which have got the better of positivism. The institutionalization of history separated an ideal history "never wholly recoverable" based on a systematic, rational and scientific pursuit of the past from a history of the "specious present" based on lived experience, memory, traditions, folklore "wishful thinking...misinformation and emotions."[26] Periodically historians were reminded of their duty to be scientific. They were warned against the "specious present" crowding their lives. On the contrary, the ancient historians used listening, observing and memory to chronicle the past. The memoirs of travellers and pilgrims depended on their experiences and stories they heard. These smaller stories became their master stories and finally the primary sources of modern historiography. Had these travellers preferred authentic, primary and written sources their memoirs would never have been written and the edited versions of these memoirs would not have entered the archive. In most cases these accounts were written after the pilgrimages ended and the pilgrims returned home. In those days memorizing experience was far more important than today because of technological reasons. Yet these accounts gained recognition as important primary sources of history. In colonial India officer-historians like James Tod and Grant Duff, manufactured the history of the Rajputs and Marathas by combining documentary and oral sources. For decades their works remained the classics of Rajput and Maratha history. Early written histories of several Indian lower castes were based on interrogations of the leaders of these castes[27]. Thus colonial ethnography produced the primary source for generations of history students[28]. These men, to paraphrase Marc Bloch's words in *The Historian's Craft*, wore sturdy shoes. They travelled widely and listened to numerous people. Grant Duff even visited France to meet Benet d'Boigne in pursuit of an authentic Maratha history. Tod's *Annals and Antiquities of Rajasthan* was based on the documents he accessed and on copious oral narratives. Native translators and interpreters assisted these colonial scholars[29]. Criticism apart, the fact that the colonial narratives were enmeshed with the oral was overlooked by Indian historians for a long time. The native element of colonial historiography makes it appear hybrid[30]. However, hybridity remains a characteristic of all knowledge including history. Historians cannot construct a past in the imagined isolation of the archive anymore because the sources available to him today could not be imagined even fifty years ago in India[31]. It is recognized that oral history, like other kinds of histories, "is a joint product shaped by both parties."[32]

The debate on the questions to be asked of respondents, their mental state, the psychological factors involved in the process of recording, the pauses and silences, the size of the sample, the editing of the recorded oral text to produce a transcript, the corroboration of sources, etc. follows the issues raised above. In this context the numerous Oral History Associations have produced an oral history method. Since the 1940s oral historians have defined their subject and sixty years of professional oral history, and the transcripts produced by its practitioners, comprise an archive of oral history which Indian historians can easily consult. Nonetheless practising oral history in India is fraught with serious problems. The technology for executing oral history is affordable but the political conditions in India inveigh against critical history. In countries where the media is corporate owned the voice of the oppressed are unlikely to be heard easily. Large parts of India are militarized to the point where recovering oral histories is difficult if not impossible. Most of the oral history readers have been produced in the West where the financial and institutional conditions for research are more favourable than in India. Indian historians, in comparison, have not written a single oral history reader suited to Indian conditions. Moreover, the learning of languages and courses in interdisciplinary social science does not command a premium in India. The denigration of history and the paucity of funds for oral history workshops have made matters worse. In Indian schools and colleges the teaching of history remains obsolete and no movement towards converting it into an interrogation aligned to the pedagogy of the oppressed is visible.

While the academic conditions in India discourage oral history the political conditions, worsened by globalization and nationalism in India, confronting researchers are formidable. The problem faced by oral historians in India is aptly expressed in the following words:

> Construction sites are spread across the city, yet they are difficult spaces to access. Security guards keep a check at entrances and visitors are not welcome. Hence, it became necessary for me to find a means to access these sites through organizations that have permission to work within them. These considerations led to my collaboration with a non-government organization (NGO) called Mobile Creches, which allowed me to visit a site in Gurgaon, where they had a long-established crèche facility, and another at Dwarka, where a fully functional crèche was not yet operational. Talking to mothers who visit the crèche to feed their babies, pick up and drop their children or to just keep an eye on them, was easier as they felt safe in the setting of a school...In Gurgaon I tried to speak to other women who did not have children to drop off or whose children did not go to the crèche, but they were afraid to communicate freely

> as they feared a supervisor or co-worker might overhear our conversation. I was warned on a couple of occasions to restrict myself to the walls of the school[33].

The patient time-consuming tape-recorded interview, based on a structured questionnaire, is called oral history to distinguish it from oral tradition by oral historians. But it is not always easy to use the tape recorder or camcorder and the "structured questionnaire" does prove problematic: "To facilitate discussions about work and family it was better practice, I discovered, to have unstructured conversations. A questionnaire or a recorder proved to be a hindrance in establishing a relationship of trust."[34] Since oral history involves living people, trust between the historian and his subjects is crucial to its success. This highlights a range of interdisciplinary activity involving individual and collective psychology. In the case of individuals who answer specific questions in front of a recorder or camera the heightened self-consciousness and self-representation may distort the truth. The recording itself is a historical and dramatic act which may insert psychological distortions into the testimony produced by it. Histories based only on oral testimonies can be as inaccurate as the ones based on written sources. Oral testimony can be as selective as a document and this complicates the task of the historian. Individual versions of an event change because different individuals remember it in different contexts. For instance, rumour, always contextual, passes into oral and written narratives. Memories change over time–they may become sweet or sour according to the conditions in which they are narrated; happy people often have happy memories and unhappy people tend to live with regrets. People reveal and hide what they wish to irrespective of the ambitions of the historian recording their speech and this highlights the time-honoured value of corroborating sources:

> As a rule, our memories romanticize the past. But when one has renounced a creed or been betrayed by a friend, the opposite mechanism sets to work. In the light of that later knowledge, the original experience loses its innocence, becomes tainted and rancid in recollection[35].

In India oral history is unorganized and is available as a dispersed form of information rarely used by historians. Indian researchers in most fields, and specially the fields of women's, peasant and working class history, use oral testimonies on a significant scale but India does not have associations which promote systematic oral history. Perhaps the only known oral history repository in India is located in the Nehru Memorial Museum and Library, Teen Murti Bhawan, New Delhi and the great majority of transcripts there have come from old freedom fighters, diplomats and political leaders. There is enormous scope for oral history in Indian schools and universities where the young must be encouraged and 'de-schooled' to think about the past with greater imagination and sensitivity. Oral history projects in schools and colleges will make students socialize with the working poor whose stories do not feature in the narrative of the nation. This socializing is important in a society where social and economic disparities are rampant. Globalization has increased the pace of urbanization and migration which create new purposes for oral history. The poor migrants, peasants and tribal people displaced by growth and development, are forgotten by the media. Only oral historians and filmmakers can rescue their histories and preserve them for future historians.

On vital issues like insurgency, counter-insurgency, social protest, agrarian distress, caste discrimination, gender discrimination, class exploitation, migration, child abuse, domestic violence, unemployment and memories of communal riots and other forms of violence oral history can, with sufficient research training, generate narratives without which no history of modern and contemporary India would be complete. Oral history is crucial to a country where the government spends only a fraction of its GDP on education and health with obvious results. Many decades ago, Marc Bloch had underscored the value of understanding people in the following words: "A little more understanding of people would be necessary merely for guidance, in the conflicts which are unavoidable; all the more to prevent them while there is yet time."[36] This overview of oral history asserts that oral testimonies might help us develop this "understanding" in a deeply divided unjust world "while there is yet time." Due to the painstaking efforts of oral historians the genre has acquired a methodological rigour and intellectual legitimacy. It has been asserted that just any recording is not oral history. The silence of the historian or his assumed innocence of human psychology cannot produce valuable oral history. Oral history, like written history, is not a monologue. It is not based on a fetish of oral testimony. Oral historians are trained historians and oral history involves a purposeful and careful recording of individual or group experiences. Oral history is the conscious product of a skilful and empathetic dialogue between the historian and the subject. Hence it is called a "conversational narrative." The oral recording, done over several hours, days or even weeks, produces a written transcript for reference to be placed in an oral history archive. Ritchie clearly states that an "interview becomes oral history only when it has been recorded, processed in some way, made available in an archive, library, or other repository, or reproduced in relatively verbatim form for publication. Availability for general research, reinterpretation, and verification defines oral history. By preserving the tapes and the transcripts of their interviews, oral historians seek to leave as complete, candid, and reliable a record as possible"[37]. The rules of written history are similar to the ones which guide oral history with perhaps one crucial distinction. The oral historian converses with the 'people without history' to check the abuse of history. His purpose of writing history is clear. He wants to document the history of people often found missing in the archives.

Concluding Remarks

The analytical treatment of oral evidence has always been important to historiography since the ancient times. Oral historians like Paul Thompson correctly assert that during the greater part of the recording of history historians did not consider oral evidence inferior to the written sources. Indeed, before the advent of professional history in the 19th century oral evidence comprised an indispensable part of the repertoire of a historian's sources. The social histories produced by Frederick Engels, Paul Thompson and E.P. Thompson demonstrate that interviews and visual observations were integral to all written narratives before their formalization in the establishments of historians. Oral histories were integral to the *historikerstreit* which re-interrogated the history of National Socialism in West Germany after the Second World War. They are also indispensable to the writing of Feminist, Labour, Dalit and Tribal histories. Nonetheless, and despite its value, oral history remains neglected in many countries because of the elitism of professional history writing. Professional historians in many countries, including India, have neglected oral history despite its growth and popularity in the 20th century. Instead of realizing and accepting the history and potential of oral history, the establishment historians have tried their best to exile it from their professional practice. Their fetish for documentary evidence has confined the discipline of history into the pedantic corridors of history departments. The neglect of oral history is more visible in a country like India where this way of producing historical narratives can reach those contemporary historical subjects upon which the historian cannot write with the help of the primary sources provided by the state manicured archive. As a well-crafted research tool and a public historical narrative open to criticism and refinement oral history can be used by the historians like the anthropologists and sociologists use their data collected during fieldwork.

This essay has demolished the distinction between the oral and the written and asserted that history is a hybrid subject. Post-1945, and especially after the student-worker rebellions of 1968 challenged the establishments in the West, oral history developed with the purpose of recording histories from 'below'[38]. Some Indian universities have been attacked by the state in the recent past and the students have responded by demonstrating their solidarity with the deprived and oppressed in Indian society. The state and media induced siege of the Jawaharlal Nehru University and Hyderabad Central University in 2016 was reminiscent of the events which rocked universities across the world in 1968. The 2016 sieges in India have produced, and will continue to produce, oral narratives which no Indian historian can ignore. The oral historians have periodically explored the problems of method, re-thought the field of oral history, re-conceptualized the way oral texts are read and interpreted and thought about the interview process and how it defines the oral testimony itself. This development of oral history since 1945 has had two consequences. One, oral history has gained recognition as an academically legitimate way of knowing the past especially of those people whose interviews are either being recorded or are available to us as transcripts stored in an oral history archive. In many countries innovative approaches to oral history at the individual and community levels have been encouraged to develop social empathy. This way of doing popular history assumes a particular significance in fast urbanizing societies in which oral traditions vanish quickly and masses of migrants risk being left out of written history. Two, the methods and problems of analysing oral testimonies have assumed widespread academic salience in consonance with the academic recognition accorded to oral history in many countries where changes in pedagogy have kept pace with historical change. These changes need not always be progressive and in fact, under globalization, they are often regressive. Further, oral history is the product of a dialogue in which speaking, listening and silences happen over time. The problems of recovering memory, dialectics of remembering and forgetting, differences and similarities between individual and collective memories, distinctions between the written accounts of events and their recollection as oral testimonies and the political conditions informing the courageous collection of oral narratives make the work of oral historians rewarding, exciting and sometimes dangerous. Finally, all history is a conversation between the historian and his sources and what is said of oral tradition is relevant to oral history:

> Oral traditions have a part to play in the reconstruction of the past. The importance of this part varies according to place and time. It is a part similar to that played by written sources

because both are messages from the past to the present, and messages are key elements in historical reconstruction. But the relationship is not one of the diva and her understudy in the opera: when the star cannot sing the understudy appears: when writing fails, tradition comes on stage. This is wrong. Wherever oral traditions are extant they remain an indispensable source for reconstruction. They correct other perspectives just as much as other perspectives correct them.[39]

NOTES

1. Nayanjot Lahiri's comments on an earlier are gratefully acknowledged.
2. *Oral Tradition As History*. Madison, Wisconsin: University of Wisconsin Press, 1985, pp. 197-98.
3. *The Sociological Imagination.* London, New York: OUP, 2000, p. 7.
4. *Oral Tradition As History*, p. xii.
5. Leopold von Ranke, *Selected Works*, Volume 3: *From Vormärz to Prussian Dominance, 1815-1866*, excerpts from *Selected Works (1824-1881)*–Introduction to Ranke's *The History of the Latin and Teutonic Nations* (1824), p. 2 [German History in Documents and Images *online*].
6. Eileen Ka-May Cheng, *Historiography: An Introductory Guide.* London: Continuum, 2012, pp. 5-60. Also see the several entries in Marnie Hughes-Warrington, *Fifty Key Thinkers on History*, Third Edition, London: Routledge, 2015.
7. *The Voice of the Past.* Oxford: OUP, 1988, pp. 57-58.
8. Ibid., p. 57; also see Sumit Sarkar, *Writing Social History*. New Delhi: OUP, 1998. He begins the book with a telling comment: "Introspection about their own location in society has not been too common among Indian historians... What is neglected is the whole question of the conditions of production and reception of academic knowledge, its relationships with different kinds of common sense. We lack, in other words, a social history of historiography."

9. *Itihaas* and *taarikh* are words which mean history in Hindi and Urdu. *Kahaani* or *mythyaa* is a work of fiction based mostly on imagination. These words refer to stories and fables.
10. The Marathi word *bakhar* is a corruption of the Arab word *khabar* which means news. The *bakhars* were based on memory and are well known sources of Maratha history. For the relationship between memory and historiography also see Prachi Deshpande, *Creative Pasts: Historical Memory and Identity in Western India 1700-1960.* New Delhi: Permanent Black, 2007.
11. On the evolution of modern historical thought among Indians see Michael Gottlob (ed.), *Historical Thinking in India.* New Delhi: OUP, 2006.
12. Partha Chatterjee and Anjan Ghosh (eds.), *History and the Present.* Ranikhet: Permanent Black, 2002, p. 12.
13. See some of his brilliant short pieces in *The End of the Peace Process.* New Delhi: Penguin, 2003.
14. According to the post-modern scholars history is an act of emplotment designed by the historian and there is not much to distinguish professional history from literature. For details see Hayden White, *Metahistory: The Historical Imagination in Nineteenth Century Europe.* John Hopkins University Press, 1973; Alun Munslow, *Deconstructing History.* Special Indian Edition, Routledge, 2007; Keith Jenkins, *At the Limits of History: Essays on Theory and Practice.* London & New York: Routledge, 2009. For a critique of the post-modern position see Anirudh Deshpande, 'Remaking the Indian Historian's Craft: The Past, Present and Future of History as an Academic Discipline', in *Economic and Political Weekly*, February 16, 2013.
15. The centrality of method to history writing, in general, to distinguish history from fiction and counter post-modern subjectivism is asserted in Simon Gunn and Lucy Faire (eds.), *Research Methods for History.* Edinburgh: Edinburgh University Press, 2012.
16. Ronald J. Grele, 'Movement without Aim–Methodological and Theoretical Problems in Oral History', in Robert Perks and Alistair Thomson, *The Oral History Reader.* London: Routledge, 1998, p. 39.

17. For example, see the case of the 43-year-old fourth grade textbook *Shivchatrapati* on Shivaji taught to impressionable children in the schools of Maharashtra–Kishore Darak, *Freezing History in Pedagogy,* Kafila.org, 25/12/2013.
18. Alistair Thompson, 'Life Stories and Historical Analysis' in *Research Methods for History*, 101-2.
19. See Chang, op. cit., passim for details.
20. For details of how this "conversational narrative" is produced see *The Oral History Reader*, op. cit., introduction.
21. *Fiction in the Archives Pardon Tales and Their Tellers in Sixteenth Century France.* Stanford: Stanford University Press, 1987.
22. The importance of the oral in Islamic learning is underlined by Karen Armstrong, *Muhammad–Prophet for Our Time.* London: Harper Press, 2006 and *Islam: A Short History.* London: Phoenix, 2006.
23. A point made forcefully in Raziuddin Aquil and Partha Chatterjee (eds.), *History in the Vernacular.* Ranikhet: Permanent Black, 2008.
24. Cheng, *Historiography*, 63.
25. *We Wish to Inform You that Tomorrow We Will be Killed with Our Families–Stories from Rwanda.* New York: Picador, 1998.
26. Paul H. Clyde and Burton F. Beers, *A History of Western Impacts and Eastern Responses, 1830-1975–The Far East.* Sixth Edition, New Delhi: Prentice Hall of India Private Limited, 1976, p. 2.
27. For an example of this see P.W. Bradbeer, 'The Role of the Kingdom of Satara in Suppressing Deccan Bunds, 1812-1832' in A.R. Kulkarni and N.K. Wagle (eds.), *Region, Nationality and Religion.* Mumbai: Popular Prakashan, 1999.
28. As an excellent example of early colonial ethnography informed by oral testimonies of the Dalit castes see Captain Alexander Mackintosh, *An Account of the Origin and Present Condition of the Tribe of Ramoshis Including the Life of the Chief Oomiah Naik.* Bombay: American Mission Press, 1833.
29. The *charans* are local, often hereditary, folklorists of Rajasthan well-versed in the history of several Rajput lineages. Their craft has been primarily oral since the medieval times.

30. For more on the impact of colonial historiography on history writing in India see Romila Thapar, *The Past as Present: Forging Contemporary Identities Through History*. New Delhi: Aleph, 2014, especially pp. 42-57.
31. A fine blend of written and oral history is to be found in Shahid Amin, *Event, Metaphor, Memory: Chauri Chaura 1922-1992.* New Delhi: Penguin, 2006.
32. Donald A. Ritchie, *Doing Oral History–A Practical Guide*. OUP, 2003, p. 30.
33. Aaradhana J. Dalmia, 'Strong Women, Weak Bodies, Muted Voices-Women Construction Workers in Delhi', *Economic and Political Weekly*, June 30, 2012, pp. 249-255.
34. Ibid.
35. Arthur Koestler in Richard H. Crossman (ed.), *The God That Failed.* New York: Columbia University Press, 2001, p. 55.
36. *The Historian's Craft*. New York: Vintage Books, 1953; Indian edition, Delhi: Aakar Books, 2017, p. 144.
37. *Doing Oral History–A Practical Guide*, p. 24.
38. For more on this see Thomas Lee Charlton, Lois E. Meyer, Rebecca Sharpless, *Handbook of Oral History.* New York: Altamira Press, 2006 *passim*. The evolution of oral history as a part of popular history is also discussed in *The Oral History Reader*, op. cit., introduction.
39. *Oral Tradition As History*, p. 199.

3

The Visual as an Archive: Questions and Answers

> During the past forty years, the range of sources in which historians claim expertise has certainly increased. It now includes place names, landscape patterns, and–for recent history–film.
>
> –John Tosh, *The Pursuit of History*, p. 72.

The title of this short essay comprises a question the likes of which we, the historians, have asked of our profession for the last hundred years. What is the purpose of writing history and what are the methods of writing it? If the archive is central to history writing what comprises the archive? In Leopold von Ranke's dictum the archive is defined in the terms set by the modern state and the historians patronized by it. According to these terms the historians' archive is strictly official, enclosed in a building and accessible to the experts whose professional work is to write history. This definition held for a long time since its inception in the 19th century. But these days this definition is not held sacrosanct although no history is possible without an archive in the same way as no product is possible without its raw materials. Speaking of history, in passing, we must note that the practice of history writing is much older than the birth of history as a modern discipline in the 19th century. It was in the 19th century that the rise of the nation-states in Europe coincided with the professionalization and institutionalization of an ancient vocation once known as an *ars historica*. This point has been made in the previous chapter. Indeed, Professor Ranke's statist definition of facts and documents, on which continues to rest the foundation of modern historiography, would have made little sense to Herodotus and Ibn Khaldun not to mention numerous others who followed in the footsteps of these inspiring men. For instance, Karl Marx and Frederick Engels had disdain for the statist historians of their time for understandable reasons. To them history meant economic and social history and a study of class struggle. Feminist critics describe the Rankean method patriarchal because he spoke of the historian, as a hero, working amongst princesses "under a curse and needing to be saved" in the archive[1]. In their view the historian casts a male gaze on archival material devouring it in a patriarchal feast. Mercifully, since the end of the 19th century, the definition of the archive has become broad enough to defy even an attempted characterization of the term. In fact, as Ludmilla Jordanova points out in an essay on the historian's approach to visual materials, "in practice some historians in each generation have wanted to think with their eyes, and they have done so in a wide range of ways."[2] The change in the definition of the archive happened in tandem with the emergence of new ways of 'doing' history, including popular and labour history, in the 20th century. In fact, the rise of the social sciences on the one hand, and the various revolutionary movements in Europe and the growing anti-colonial movements in the colonies on the other, expanded the subject horizon of the historians in America and Europe. The term thinking with our eyes reminds us of what Bloch wrote in the *Historian's Craft*. In his view, which all city-based historians must take seriously today, acquiring a pair of sturdy shoes and walking in the countryside is as important to write history as the documentary archive.

These days we speak of the documentary archives, the oral archives, the visual archives, cinema archives, feminist archives, community archives, Holocaust archives, oral tradition archives, folklore archives, military archives, partition archives and who knows how many other archives. In sum, no source is anathema to the revolutionary historians and they seem most ardent in embracing every intellectual 'turn' in the social sciences. The work of historians associated with the *Historikerstreit* (the historians' quarrel) during the 1980s in Germany and the Subaltern Studies in India at the same time proves this beyond a shadow of doubt. The monumental work of the oral historian and folklorist Komal Kothari must also be mentioned here and needs greater attention in another paper. In sum, the days of not paying attention to the visual sources of history are gone and hopefully will never return and no history department in the world today is complete without a few art historians who teach visual history. Cinema history is taught in most competent contemporary universities across the world. Nonetheless in India, which has the largest film industry in the world, the subject of cinema history languishes for lack of proper academic attention.

In this context the question to be answered is simple. Should the historians consider the visual materials produced in the past and present on par with the other sources or should they treat the abundance of visual evidence present in society and the visual archives differently? According to Hayden White, one of the foremost critics of the Ranke type meta-history, photographs can help the historian produce a credible story called 'Historiophoty'. Even if we suppose White is right the important question remains partially answered because the historian remains central to the task of creating a narrative based on visual material and therefore his interpretation continues to impinge on his use of historical materials, visuals included. Even a valid narrative of the past woven with photographs cannot do without captions and hence the written narrative retains its salience in visual history. What therefore is produced is a dialectics of the written and visual. No one in his right mind can imagine good cinema without an acceptable script, and scripts are written not merely imagined. Therefore the historical context of the script remains salient to a historical understanding of cinema. In the ultimate analysis, the historians convert a collection of visuals into an archive with respect to both, written and visual history. Historians have done this for centuries and will continue to do so despite the irritation such things cause to some of their less heterodox colleagues. In recent times historians of art and architecture have written and spoken increasingly of the cultural hybridity of our pre-nationalist pasts on the basis of the penetrative insights evident in their study of temples, motifs, religious symbols, seals and visualization of cross regional epics[3].

It is generally presumed that the mass printed visual began to play a particular ideological role in the construction of historical narratives in Europe after the invention of the movable printing press by the engraver, inventor and printer Johannes Gutenberg in the mid-15th century. In due course the Gutenberg Revolution changed the religious and secular mental landscape of Europe during the Renaissance and Reformation of the 16th century. In the era of colonialism and imperialism contiguous with the rise of mercantilism and modern steam-driven industry this European mental landscape became filled with an imagery which paid homage to the conquest of distant lands and their enslavement by the various European powers. Historians tend to agree that the printing press and its eventual control by the European ruling classes led to the creation of a print culture not only in Europe but across the world which became increasingly enmeshed with it from the period which began with the Spanish conquest of America CE 1500 onwards. The Europeans carried and established the printing presses practically everywhere they settled and with the press came the imagery of Christianity and the penny press. Images from Europe were transmitted to the colonies through illustrated texts and from the colonies to Europe in similar fashion. This exchange of visuals proved influential in the creation of colonial and metropolitan stereotypes in the long run; both the fetishized Orient and Occident would derive sustenance from this imagery. Ultimately, as scholars like Benedict Anderson have pointed out, the print culture within which the visual as an aid to text was embedded, shaped the historical imagination of millions in

Europe and its colonies and thereby affected mentalities almost universally. The impact of the artist-created visual on social attitudes towards religion, culture, sex, travel, seafaring, nature and the 'self' and 'other' is well documented in historiography. For instance, and increasingly from the 15th century, popular attitudes towards religious and secular matters in general were reproduced in the imagery contained in what came to be called the penny press; a historical precursor of today's social media. Visual pornography, the native, the plantation, the slave and the colonial-colonized landscape appeared early in this imagery which reinforced and spread the masculine and patriarchal attitudes prevalent in European societies[4]. Visual documentation and the consumption of images went together with the development of modern colonialism and imperialism. This function of the visual, both fake and real, as information and archive, remains important in our contemporary times.

While the connection between an ever growing visual archive, Western power and knowledge seems well established in our narration of it, we must pause and examine the visual as an archive of perceived reality and mentality in non-European and pre-modern contexts as well. Egyptologists, for example, piece together a history of Ancient Egypt with the aid of visuals carved on the Pyramids and Temples built by their ancestors in the Nile Valley several thousand years ago. In Egypt the visuals commissioned by the Pharaohs and the nobles, and mercifully explained by the hieroglyphic script, narrate a story of monarchy, conquest, religious beliefs and social life. No social history of ancient Egypt or events like the defeat of the Hittites by the great Pharaoh Ramses or the marriage and worship of the kings is complete without a reference to the visuals left behind as indelible records in stone by the ancient Egyptians. Ancient Indian temples are similar in import. For instance, the visuals carved on Kailash, Khajuraho or Konark are narrations best left to the interpretations of art historians. In Sarnath and Sanchi are found carved frescoes which illustrate the stories present in the Buddhist canonical texts. Similarly, in the rock cut and illustrated Ajanta Caves the sculptors, architects, donors, traders and painters have left behind an invaluable visual archive for posterity. Often the existence and survival of these temples and excavated caves is testimony to the technology used by their creators several centuries before the Industrial Revolution made humanity conscious of the concept of technology. In Konark the creators made huge statues of the domesticated Indian elephant as a visual tribute to an animal without whose power and intelligence the construction of this massive temple would have been impossible. Available contemporaneous treatises on the construction of Konark describe stone-lifting techniques to which the draught power of the Indian elephant remained central.

Painting, another form of visual source, was not the monopoly of Europe. In medieval India, and especially during the Mughal period and the 18th century, paintings were produced across the Indian subcontinent on a variety of subjects and by all means comprise an archive the student of Indian history cannot afford to ignore. In this endeavour the Mughal monarchs and nobility were quite active and so were the rajas and nawabs of the various principalities of India. Over time various schools of painting evolved in India with distinctive features. The traditions continued in the Princely States during the 19th century and, till photography began to replace portraits and artistic visual representations from the mid-19th century onwards, created an archive to be read alongside other historical sources. In pre-colonial China, South East Asia and the Far East too the practice of illustrating the past with help of visuals was well established. So we actually observe a vast international visual archive created in the pre and post-Gutenberg Revolution in areas which did not have a print culture or colonial ideology. Much of the material contained in this pre-colonial informal archive reappeared in the ideological framework of tourism from the late 19th century as the European gaze on the non-European subjugated world intensified. In several instances the pieces of art comprising this precolonial heritage were expropriated and deposited in the libraries and archives in the West to the advantage of scholars located there. Thus the connection between modern Western colonialism and the repositories of visual materials built up in the centres of research in the West since the 18th century cannot be overlooked in any study of the evolution of the visual archive.

There is no reason to restrict our discussion of the visual as an archive to the historical period. Pre-literate societies were the pioneers of visual art and records; many of these traditions of a visual narration of the past were inherited by literate communities as civilisation developed. A lot of what passes as tribal art in our times comprises this visual archive. The need to preserve and transmit human knowledge emerged at a time when humanity diverged from the animal world with the aid of imagination and an erect spine. To begin with, the urge to paint and engrave on the stone walls of the caves temporarily inhabited by the hunter gatherers was caused by the inherent human tendency to leave behind a record for posterity. Many paintings might have been produced by the older or infirm members of the hunting communities who stayed back in the caves while the young foraged for food. Social experience was embodied in the task of painting or else how did the painters know the use of dyes or stone tools? What made them use colours which were supposed to have a long life? What was the chemical composition of these colours? Obviously the cave painting is a rich multifarious archive of a way of life. In fact the visual as an archive was first created by pre-historic societies as the cave paintings of Bhimbetka, to take only an example, tell us. Vignettes of Paleolithic life, remarkably preserved over thousands of years, appear with an astonishing clarity in these paintings. I remember being gifted one of them reproduced on a vitrified tile at the Indian History Congress in Bhopal in December 2001. The etching is that of a funeral. The grave is marked as a circle with stakes being put in by a man or woman. The circle is virtual and also to be understood as a metaphor of the life cycle of birth, life and death. Next to the grave are two grieving almost inconsolable members of the large family. The grave contains either a whole family or a smaller section of the community comprising three adults, a child and a domestic animal which appears to be a dog, an animal used as a hunting assistant and guard since time immemorial. The dog might have been buried alive unconscious or killed before being buried with its masters; a practice common to many prehistoric and ancient cultures. In Egypt the domestic animals and slaves were slain and buried with their masters in the hope of life after death. In sum the Bhimbetka painting represents an entire paleolithic way of life. Other paintings show various animals and hunting scenes; the depiction of flora and fauna in such paintings comprise crucial traces of a past eventually overrun by civilisation and geography. Speaking of geography and geographical history, a pet theme of Fernand Braudel and his followers, the visual imagery easily becomes an archive documenting historical change. The changing course of rivers, the drying up and shrinking of glaciers, the disappearance of forest cover and the effect of urbanization on the environment are well documented by photographs, films and satellite images. Thus the list of the raw material of history keeps expanding in keeping with the growing demands of time. In most instances the character of the visual as an archive in aid of critical historical narration is impeccable. Much extrapolation can easily follow the observations made on the basis of such 'hard' evidence.

All this suggests that the visual turn in history preceded the invention of the camera and the movie camera in the nineteenth century. The camera, to begin with, did not produce an image of reality very different from the one reproduced in a good realistic painting. For example, da Vinci's Mona Lisa of the 16th century is as good a picture as the photographs of Balzac or his contemporaries shot by a camera in the 1840s. Good colour paintings are often as good as photographs; both convey objective reality and the subjective perception of the creators simultaneously. Photography and cinematography increased the volume and variety of still and moving images in society exponentially as time passed. There is a certain contemporaneity in photographs which a painting may lack; the latter can easily be a reproduction of reality with the aid of memory which itself may be impressionistic. For example, a painting of a scene is drawn over a certain period of time by the painter even as the scene keeps changing in front of him. The equivalent of this is a series of photographs which captures this change frame by frame.

From the 1840s a large and variegated cache of visual material was produced worldwide but the historians were slow to realize its historical potential. Whereas earlier the artists took time to produce images the camera operated instantly to photograph slaves, plantations, tribals, workers, plants, animals, intellectuals, monarchs, professionals and almost everything which inhabited the modern industrial and colonial world. Family albums began to proliferate. Studio photography developed in Europe and the colonies converting the photograph into a statement of social identity. Camera tricks, a precursor of the contemporary fake visual news, evolved in tandem with the exponential development in photography. Wars, disasters and social life were photographed and later filmed extensively. The Crimean War, American Civil War and the Indian Revolt of 1857 *inter alia* have left behind a rich collection of photographs which historians later used to good effect in their narrations of these events and the Great War became the first major war to be extensively filmed.

The Great War documentary footage became available to the public soon after 1918 and drove home the truth that modern war was anything but heroic. Thanks to the enormous footage and photos produced of the war most Europeans became unenthusiastic about war in the 1920s and 1930s. Unfortunately Fascist and Nazi propaganda trumped this realization in the 1920s and 1930s; war was heroic to these ideologies. Films were crucial to the rise of both movements. At the same time the Bolshevik Revolution was extensively photographed and filmed and no one can forget the inspiring work of Sergei Eisenstein in this context. By the time the Spanish Civil War (1936-39) and the Second World War (1939-45) happened, both still cameras and movie cameras had become technologically advanced enough to create a visual war archive which historians to this date use. State propaganda photographs and films was another matter which attracted the masses and critics in equal measure in all countries. Cameras were sold in large numbers in the colonies where both the ruling colonizers and the protesting colonial subjects used them to further opposing agendas; photographs and films became central to imperialism and nationalism in the colonies. In most countries the film studio was equipped with paraphernalia needed by the clients who wished to appear as what they were not in the photos taken by expert photographers. In sum, by the time the Second World War ended literally billions of photographs had been taken and hundreds of thousands of films, documentaries and others, made. The historians had a visual archive at their disposal and this archive had the potential of enriching their craft in new ways. There is one obvious way in which this has happened. The visuals often become the starting point of questions which lead to hypotheses and thereby new directions in research. The descriptive power of the visual, if missing in written history, provokes young minds into asking new questions of their subjects.

In order to use the visual archives historians must depart from the primary motive of modern establishment history which, in general, is a narration of the "formation and legitimation of the nation state."[5] Once this task is accomplished the historian's approach to historiography becomes open ended. We then speak more of approaches and learning from other approaches than the more narrowly defined methods with the tag of specialization attached to them because no discipline really has an exclusive method. The historians must select visual materials in accordance with the topic of their research and verify their authenticity. Like a biologist or geologist they must see, observe, describe and dissect these materials repeatedly and carefully. Only a few viewings of the visual are never enough to dovetail it into a narrative; repeated viewings reveal new aspects of the visual. The historians must look at both the material world and mental attitudes presented by the creator of the visual or the cameraman in a studio because no image is strictly objective in orientation and no film is really complete outside its context. The questions who, why, how and when remain important in the historians' interaction with the visual world in the same way as they do in an archive or library or interview. The mere presence of the visual material inside a visual archive or outside might change the orientation of history but it does not change the practice of history as a craft the main purpose of which is to achieve a credible reconstruction of the past based on verifiable evidence. Nothing remains outside the purview of the interdisciplinary context of history and critically using visual materials in our workshop improves our craftsmanship and makes us "better" historians. As Jordanova says: "It is plausible to take a self-aware, yet innocent stance: so much evidence survives that counts as 'visual materials', and visual experience has played such a central role in all aspects of the past, that it would be perverse not to use their possibilities. We should do so in a manner that both respects the general code of practice for deploying any source and takes account of specialist knowledge."[6] Since the historian does not deploy any source uncritically his approach to the visual will be as critical as it is towards the written or oral.

Therefore, while considering visual material as a source of history the historian must be aware of the following:

1. The social, economic and cultural context of the visual material being examined. The value of corroborating the visual material with other historical source material remains crucial here as a time-tested method of writing verifiable and authentic history.
2. The biography of the creator of the visual evidence is crucial in the same measure as a statesman creating an official document. His or her ideological leanings, record of authenticity and overall trustworthiness must be assessed by the historian. The production of the visual must be seen as a part of the overall work of the creator in question.
3. In case of cinema the examination of the script remains important. Is the script based on a historical or literary text and how close is it to narrating an objective well rounded story of the past? If cinema claims historical authenticity the veracity of this claim must be examined carefully by the film historian. Alternatively, if cinema is fantasy the

cultural objective of this fantasy must be analysed by the film historian.

4. In case of documentary films, the authenticity of the locales and objects being highlighted by the filmmaker merit the special attention of the historian in addition to the objective of the documentary and the script employed by the documentary maker. Since most good documentaries use a variety of historical sources in their narration these public sources themselves call for the historians' attention.
5. Wherever possible the historian must endeavour to access the full footage the edited version of which is presented to the audience as cinema by the filmmaker. This will enable the historian to examine aspects left out of the film deliberately by the director and such extra material may contain extra historical information for the historian. Here the role of the film archive is important because only a film archive might contain the unedited footage of a film.

In sum, therefore, if used meticulously any authentic visual sources in corroboration with available oral and written sources opens up numerous possibilities for writing myriad exciting and critical histories. Film is particularly relevant to the writing and re-writing of recent history and here the historians can learn a lot from socially sensitive journalists and photographers.

NOTES

1. Simon Gunn and Lucy Faire (eds.), *Research Methods for History*. Edinburgh: Edinburgh University Press, 2012, p. 17.
2. 'Approaching Visual Materials', in Simon Gunn and Lucy Faire (eds.), *Research Methods for History*. Edinburgh: Edinburgh University Press, p. 33.
3. A recent example of such exciting scholarship is Dhar, Parul Pandya, 2020. "Art in Translation: Interpreting Icons and Narratives across the Indian Ocean," in ASEAN and India: Partners of Integration in Asia. Proceedings of the 5th Roundtable of the ASEAN-India Network of Think Tanks (AINTT),

Jakarta, 2018, ed. AIC-RIS. New Delhi: Asean-India Centre at Research & Information Systems for Developing Countries (AIC-RIS).

4. Eric Berkowitz, *Sex and Punishment: 4000 Years of Judging Desire.* London: The Westbourne Press, 2013.
5. *Research Methods for History*, Introduction, p. 16.
6. Ibid., p. 45.

4

Fiction and History: Some Possibilities

> You were Mewar's and my great hope... You were meant for greater things. Highness. You have it in you to be the greatest Rajput ruler the country has seen. You have the vision and wiliness to beat all our enemies and become Maharana of the whole of India. Can you break with your wife? Only then will you be able to get the better of your brother and his mother and concentrate on Babur and our other enemies.
>
> –Quoted from the last letter to Maharaj Kumar from Kausalya, his wet nurse and mistress, *Cuckold*, 598-600.

Following the lines of inquiry laid down in the preceding chapters this essay examines the academic potential of historical fiction.[1] It is based on a close reading of the late Kiran Nagarkar's historical novel *Cuckold*, which is set in medieval north India. Throughout the article some parts of *Cuckold* have been used as historical reference points to arrive at positions pertinent to Indian history in general and military history in particular. The paper is also an attempt to contextualize *Cuckold* and highlight its salience in the theoretical reconstruction of Indian military history attempted therein. On the whole, this intervention underlines the stimulus given to written history by well-conceived, properly researched and elegantly written historical fiction. Having said this, I hasten to add that the argument that historical fiction inspires written history or the social sciences can be extended in equal measure to good fiction of any kind. Since fiction is located at the intersection of history and imagination its ability to raise questions and inspire research can hardly ever be underestimated. Given the contemporary circumstances in which history as a subject is contracting and general interest in it is declining one hopes this kind of inspiration generates a wider, and more critical, awareness of our past.

When the novel *Cuckold* was published it got a few reviews. A good one was written by the late Khushwant Singh in *Outlook*. This made me buy the book and my interaction with the novel and interest in historical fiction finally culminated in an earlier draft of this essay. Had *Cuckold* won the Booker or Pultizer Prize it would undoubtedly be better known if not actually more widely read. It is a long book and in parts too detailed and dragging. In my view Nagarkar should have written a shorter book. On February 23, 2001 the city supplement of the *Hindustan Times* of Delhi did us the favour of carrying a small report on the novel and its modest author. This report, like some of the reviews I read, contained two errors. Firstly, it called *Cuckold* the story of the Maharaj Kumar, the elusive husband of the historical and legendary Bhakti saint Mirabai. Secondly it misquoted Nagarkar by confusing the battles of Panipat and Khanua. Could the author of *Cuckold* have said that Rana Sanga and Babur fought at Panipat in 1526? The First Battle of Panipat, as all students of Indian history know, was fought between Babur and Ibrahim Lodi. According to the writer of this report, to claim that *Cuckold* is only the story of Maharaj Kumar is like suggesting that *War and Peace* is only a narration of events in the life of Count Bezukhov. It is true that the Maharaj Kumar is the cuckold in the novel and is metaphorically cuckolded by none other than Lord Krishna. But the canvas of the novel is much larger. It is an imaginary reconstruction of life, as it must have been, in medieval Mewar considered the jewel of Rajputana, based on meticulous research by Nagarkar who was a Maharashtrian. It is a story as much of Maharana Sangram Singh and his times as it is of his family and kingdom. Novels like *Cuckold* cannot be reduced to simplified interpretations. It is a pity that such a work does not command larger attention in a country with a rich historical legacy. Indeed, our media's attention to historical events reproduces the cavalier attitude of most Indians towards history. It is my contention that fiction has the potential of making historical subjects interesting. It can offer a path to serious academic history which, to begin with, intimidates the more curious amongst us. In this context, Nagarkar's novel offers a refreshing way of looking at the past, especially in an inter-disciplinary way.

Cuckold is much more than a narration of the events and experiences in the life of the Maharaj Kumar, the elder son and heir apparent of Rana Sanga the king of Mewar. It is an emotive account of the history of Mewar, mostly presented from the viewpoint of the Maharaj Kumar, the hero of the novel. The political character of the prince Maharaj Kumar is essentially conceived as a counter to the milieu of feudal India with all its possibilities and problems. At places he reminds you of Muhammad-bin-Tughluq and at many places in the novel his attitude towards military and other matters are highlighted deliberately in contrast to feudal practice. By reconstructing the military experiments of the Maharaj Kumar, Nagarkar is able to critically examine the martial mentality prevalent in medieval Rajputana. This underscores the importance of examples to the study of military history and theory, as mentioned by Clauzewitz, the modern philosopher of war. This dictum has been put to good use in *Cuckold*. Since war is a human activity like social, economic and political activities its conduct is never free from the influence of social mentality. In fact, military history is often not much more than the examination of the dialectics of mentality and military activity. In this connection, *Cuckold* is an admirable commentary on the mentality of the warlike Rajputs, the heroes of nationalist histories in India. Much of this commentary is conveyed to the reader of the novel through the complex, contextualized, imagined and potentially progressive character of the Maharaj Kumar, about whom historians actually know very little. The very fact that so little is known of the Maharaj

Kumar has given Nagarkar the freedom to create his protagonist in his own image. All historians understand the difficulty of writing history without interfering personally in the task.

This chapter is not a general discourse on Nagarkar's acclaimed historical novel: rather it concentrates on the military aspects of feudal Mewar presented in *Cuckold*. Nagarkar has deftly illuminated the strengths and weaknesses of Rajputs, a first class "martial race" of north India as defined by the colonial military authorities. But he is not the first to have done so. His sources include chroniclers of the 16th century and historians like Tod, Lane-Poole and Ishwari Prasad. The scholarly works of Kasim Farishta as translated by John Briggs, Abul Fazal as translated by David Price and contemporary historians like Satish Chandra and Stephen Rosen give us a good idea of military practices existing in medieval India. But somehow historical fiction stirs the imagination unlike some types of academic history. While reading the exciting books by G.A. Henty and W.E. Johns in school, it was difficult for us to grasp the overall intellectual potential of fiction. The theoretical and philosophical realms lying beyond the domain of imagined chivalry remained largely unexplored in the genre represented by authors like Henty and Johns. Compared with books like *Cuckold*, their very English perspective on European and World history does appear ideologically biased to the post- and counter-colonial scholar. But despite their limitations they have the ability to stoke the imagination of their adolescent readers. For a long time when I was in junior school, I remember, the exploits of Bigglesworth (the RAF pilot in Johns' novels) kept up my interest in the history of the two world wars. However, the overall theoretical and philosophical concerns of *Cuckold*, not to mention its multifarious military implications, make it a mature, and superior, novel in many ways. Long after you have put it down after having read and re-read sections from it, the scenes conjured up by the author haunt your imagination. The questions keep coming back, pushing you deeper into comparative history.

As far as Indian military history is concerned, *Cuckold* reiterates the combination of individual courage with the freezing of the

Indian way of warfare in medieval India. This freezing seems to have occurred in the ancient period although it appears most visibly in medieval India. According to Rosen's well-conceived volume, the ferocity of individual warriors was the chief characteristic of ancient and medieval Indian armies compared with the organization and cohesion of armies brought into India by invaders from Alexander onwards. In the Ancient World, according to Rosen, two army models seemed to have emerged. The first was the professional army which became cohesive due to the long campaigns it undertook. These armies, like those of the Spartans and Macedonians and the Roman Legions, were divorced from their societies by means of military training, traditions, messing, campaigns etc. The second model was the largely temporary "militia-type" army produced by Indian society. These visually and statistically intimidating armies had a low degree of cohesion and, as a consequence, were usually defeated by smaller professional armies in pitched battles. A typical case of such a contest was the Battle of Jhelum between Alexander and Porus fought in 326 BC. Moreover, Rosen's framework suggests that the tactics adopted by an army depended upon the model it represented. The ancient Greeks and Romans had great faith in their spear-wielding infantry phalanx and used it as their main arm of attack and defence. The cavalry, contrary to popular opinion, was deployed in a fashion meant to outflank and confound the enemy: its job was to assist the infantry. In contrast to this, the Indians relied on war elephants and charioteers. Records indicate that on the battlefield[2] there was minimal tactical coordination between the elephants, chariots, cavalry and infantry. Contemporary observers noticed how the charioteers normally did not assist the labouring infantry and vice-versa. The elephants were generally deployed to protect masses of infantry from enemy attacks. But this stratagem backfired. When attacked, the elephants often turned upon their own massed infantry, triggering a wave of confusion, demoralization and desertion.

Upon reading the account of the Battle of Khanua towards the end of *Cuckold*, the reader is struck by the coexistence of bravery in men like Rana Sanga and his ally Hasan Khan Mewati with the military stasis prevalent in medieval India. Or else by the exemplary courage of Porus in the lost Battle of Jhelum, or of Ibrahim Lodi in the First Battle of Panipat (1526), or even Sadashiv Rao 'Bhau' in the Third Battle of Panipat (1761). It becomes difficult not to believe from this marked opposition of personal courage and military stasis that Indian military tradition, as cherished and borne by its ruling elites, was unproductive and even futile. The sustained combination of individual courage and group military failures in Indian history compels you to go beyond the battlefields in search of causes. Perhaps the answers can be found in what Nagarkar, in the voice of the Maharaj Kumar, calls the classic formation of the Indian armies of yore. This involved an excessive reliance on war-elephants–often with disastrous battlefield consequences. The elephant looks intimidating but is a difficult animal to control and use effectively, especially against artillery. If the *mahaawat* was speared or shot, the elephant was prone to panic, and trampled the men plodding and pushing along behind it. Further, sitting in the *howdah* of an elephant, like Vishwas Rao during the Third Battle of Panipat in 1761, a commander provided an easy target to a sniper. The *Kshatriya* Hindu Raja, eminently exposed to the enemy in his splendid *howdah*, was himself the cause of many Indian defeats. The moment he vanished from his caparisoned elephant, the army deserted. In sum, a semi-circle of war-elephants protecting a tightly packed army comprising cavalry and mostly untrained infantry was the classical battle formation of the Hindu ruling elite. The aim of the astrologer-assisted Hindu military elite was to use this mass as a battering ram. Defeat and retreat were almost invariably never thought of and retreats were usually routs. A battle, in general, was considered decisive and not part of a long drawn strategy against a powerful enemy. The trumpeting elephants were used, I suspect, to produce a psychological effect on the enemy and sometimes they succeeded. The upper caste cavalry, unlike armies following the Greek method, briefly surveyed earlier, rushed into brief inconclusive charges. Is it possible that the infantry could not be used as a cohesive arm because of the caste system? Was the infantry shielded and kept apart because the *Kshatriya* Raja could not trust the heterogeneous masses? Possibly the infantry could not stand shoulder-to-shoulder because the armies lacked unity, training, common messing and, above all, camaraderie born of shared military experience. The differences between a largely temporary, "militia-type" army and a professional army can be analysed in this context even with contemporary overtones.

But the amazing fact is the longevity of this deployment despite its proven inefficacy. In the period covered by *Cuckold* and during the Mughal rule in India, twice at Panipat and once at Khanua, the same deployment was resorted to with similar results. The Mughals won both these battles. Surely, the refusal to learn from contemporary history is strange for battle-hardened kingdoms, led by a ruling elite immersed in martial traditions.[3] What could be the cause of this unwillingness to change? The caste system? Superstitions? An excessive reliance on Brahmin astrologers? There are several hypotheses. While discussing this inability to learn from historical events the timing of *Cuckold's* publication should also be noticed. Here, taking the liberty of travelling freely in time, I am referring to the peculiar problems besetting India at the beginning of the 21st century. The widespread tendency of not learning lessons from history can be perceived all around us. The resurgence of religious intolerance and the growing popularity of vaastu, astrology, faith healing and charlatan "gurus" makes a sharp distinction between a people aware of their past and a people trying to escape into it. In a country where millions believe that their ancient ancestors possessed airplanes and missiles where is the impulse to learn from rational history? To a historian studying military phenomena in the context of "war and society" the military establishment and popular attitudes towards it represent crucial elements of the social formation to which it belongs. As Rosen asserts: "If someone wants to theorize about Indian society and Indian military power, the understanding of Indian society that drives the theory must be set forth and justified." [1996: Preface]

Cuckold opens a window to the integrated lessons of war and history in this context.

We concentrate on two events described in vivid detail in *Cuckold*. The first is the war against Gujarat which brings out the importance of military training and cooperation among social allies in a warlike situation. The second is the widely discussed and decisive Battle of Khanua. In the first instance, during Mewar's war against Gujarat, Maharaj Kumar is shown carrying out certain experiments in mobile warfare with the help of his Rajput and Bhil friends. The involvement of the Bhils, who are organized and led by Puraji Kika, their intrepid and cunning Raja, in a campaign against the well-equipped Gujarat forces is construed deliberately by Nagarkar to highlight the military possibilities inherent in inter-caste cooperation in medieval India. Shades of the hardy Mavalas mobilized by Shivaji in the Sahyadris in the 17th century can also be perceived in this connection. From the Bhils, Nagarkar's protagonist learns the art of a people's war, comprising tested components like surprise, masquerade, feinting, quick dispersal and rapid concentration of forces. This tells us that alternate methods of war were being practised by non-Rajput warriors like the Bhils, in the forests and hills of medieval India. However, this potential for developing mobile warfare remained unexploited in feudal India for a variety of reasons. When the time comes, Maharaj Kumar conducts war against Gujarat using all the means at his disposal. Finally, a marsh, towards which the enemy cavalry is forced to flee, is used to trap and destroy the Gujaratis. But the hidebound Rajputs of Mewar do not learn a lesson from this campaign to develop a new strategy of warfare. Court intrigue, which also plays on Rana Sanga's vanity, puts paid to Maharaj Kumar's experiments and denigrates his success against Gujarat. The Rajputs, Nagarkar's novel reasserts, knew how to fight and die for their notions of honour but they seemed to have drawn very few lessons on how to win at their favourite pastime. It is not surprising that the historian's search for the wisdom of a Tsun Tzu or Clausewitz among their archives yields nothing. The bards sing of glory and this glory passed into historiography. Consequently, the history of Rajasthan became the poverty-stricken history of the Rajputs who, rationally speaking, did not learn much from their own history. First they were defeated by the fast moving Turks and later the gunpowder-using Mughals.

The experiments in warfare against Gujarat, described in vivid detail in *Cuckold*, have their limitations considering the historical period in which Nagarkar locates them. Both artillery and matchlocks are conspicuously absent from the campaign. This absence of firepower is noticed once again when the grand Rajput army leaves for Agra to confront Babur. The hundred thousand strong Mewar army, which marches out of Chittor to turn the tide of history, is shown to contain only a hundred matchlockmen and almost no artillery. Imagine how unsuccessful Mewar would have been in its campaign against Gujarat, in the fictional account given by Nagarkar, in the absence of the swamp. Personal bravery plays a role too. In a defining moment of the war with Gujarat, the Maharaj Kumar resorts to a masquerade to kill the Gujarati commander at great personal risk. He tries everything successfully against Gujarat–surprise, tactical manoeuvre, grouping and regrouping, and finally the annihilation of enemy leadership and forces. But is this possible against a seasoned artillery commander like Babur who read history and drew lessons from the battles won by the Ottomans against the Persians by the systematic use of cannons? The Gujaratis and Mewaris were alike. Babur was different.

Given its military experience, Mewar had the potential to institute regular training and planning, and to execute war exercises simulating the conditions of real war, in and around Chittor. The small anecdote of the Maharaj Kumar's visit to the Institute of Advanced Military Tactics and Strategy in Chittor should be seen in this context. (There is no historical evidence of this.) The Prince is "keen to enlarge the scope of the Institute to encompass the latest technologies" based on the "vague rumours of advances made by the Arabs, Turks and Portuguese in war materials...." Maharaj Kumar notices that the "mechanics of retreat" are not taught at the Institute, and is made to prophetically say that "if the art of retreat is studied scientifically, you'll not only reduce loss of life dramatically, you may also live to fight another war."

This is obviously Nagarkar speaking in 16th century Chittor. We know that Babur's life was a testimony to this adage. He had been defeated and hounded out of Farghana twice by the Uzbegs and always kept a rear guard ready during his battles. In comparison, the idea of retreat was anathema to the Rajputs. Their practices like wearing the *kesari bana* before the last sally and the fearful *jauhar* of their women testified to their do-or-die attitude. These practices have been glorified in written history, myths and cinema but glorification can only bring you solace not historical victory.

Was the refusal of the Rajputs to observe contemporary reality, grasp its implications and thereby develop a new synthesis of theory and practice, predicated upon the caste system? Rosen draws our attention to the relationship between Indian military weaknesses and caste. It is suggested that in the 9th and 10th centuries, rising Hindu conservatism and caste rigidity contributed to the easy fall of border territories to small groups of Turkish invaders. This often "led Hindu elites to regard the people of the border territories, who had become racially and culturally mixed, as 'repugnant' to Hindu sensibilities and not deserving of assistance..." [1996: 117] This may not be an unproductive way of looking at Indian history. But plausible answers can also be sought in the peculiarities of regional feudalism, which spawned a frog-in-the-well mentality in Indian society during the medieval period. This mentality was nurtured by the highly insular Brahminical system as noted by scholar-travellers like Al-Biruni in the 11th century.[4]

Long before the Battle of Khanua, the Ghaznavid and Ghurid invasions drove home the point that the Indian dependence on numerical superiority on the battlefield created problems for their troops. The Second Battle of Tarain fought between Prithviraj Chauhan and Mohammad Ghori in 1192 has been accurately described by Satish Chandra as "more a war of movement than a position." The Battle of Chandawar fought against Jaichand's massive army two years later for supremacy over the Gangetic plain was similar. The Turks were renowned for using mounted archers in rapid outflanking movements. Earlier, speed of movement had also given the edge to the Turks led by Saladin against the heavily armed and slower European knights during the Crusades. We must examine these facts in the context of the training imparted to the Mewar soldiers by Maharaj Kumar and his innovative friends. However, when we look at what was happening in Europe during the 16th century, the medievalism of the Rajputs assumes a new dimension.

All history and especially military history is comparative history.

Over the 16th century, a "military revolution", a concept used by Geoffrey Parker, gathered momentum in some states of Europe. This development, which was concurrent with the Renaissance and Reformation, comprised two momentous changes in warfare. Firstly, the importance of a well-drilled infantry in the armies of certain European states grew in proportion to that of the cavalry. Moreover, in time, this infantry began to use muskets on an exponentially increasing scale, and by the 17th century, the infantry square, the well-organized system of marching, back-marching and volley fire had emerged. This had the potential of breaking the best of cavalry charges. Secondly, the importance of artillery and its variety developed in tandem with the development of the infantry. While heavy artillery diminished the importance of medieval fortifications, the growth of mobile and light artillery progressively reduced the role of the cavalry in battles fought in the open. Since the infantry was also vulnerable to firepower, there was a move to introduce greater discipline in order to withstand losses. The growing reliance on firepower translated into constantly improving the design and accuracy of firearms, artillery pieces and types of ordnance used on land and sea. These developments comprised the basis of European military superiority over non-European regions from the 16th century onwards. For lack of time, I am not delving into the details of the productive development of artillery for use at sea, and consequent developments in naval strategy and tactics, which were occurring almost simultaneously. However, the "military revolution" had broader implications. It encompassed all military activities of the state like recruitment, supply and provisioning, military production, creation of uniforms and the regimental system, constant drilling and training and, above all, the development of institutions, academies, theories and a philosophy dedicated to the study of war. By the 17th century, war in Europe had become increasingly de-personalized and hand-to-hand combat was becoming rare. Personal courage was still important to prevent the infantry square from breaking under enemy fire, but the age of feudal chivalry involving individual jousting was over.

The use of firepower was not unique to Europe. In the 15th century, the Persians and Turks of Central Asia also started using artillery and personal firearms on a substantial scale. To the north of Afghanistan, the descendants of Changez and Timur were grafting firepower on to tactical mobility, a process which some Mongols had mastered. The addition of mobile and swivel artillery pieces to the system of using cavalry as a tactical reserve [here I am referring to the Mongol maneouvre called *tulughma*] was quietly ushering in a minor "military revolution" in the Ottoman territories and Central Asia. By the 15th century, the Ottoman Turks seemed to have overcome the problem of nomadic tribal divisiveness and rebelliousness by means of developing a centralized state apparatus. This state was dependent on the Christian Slave Janissaries who formed a standing professional army of around 10,000, separated from Ottoman society and beholden to the Sultan for its position. With the help of this professional army the Ottoman Sultans successfully curbed the power of the rural and religious elites for a considerable period of time. In the 15th and 16th centuries, the Ottoman Empire was at its peak and its influence was felt from Central Asia to Eastern Europe. Its military methods were well known in Iran and areas now covered by Uzbekistan and Turkmenistan.

Babur had mastered the new forms of warfare before the First Battle of Panipat. The references to *firingi* and *zarbzan* shots in the *Baburnamah* confirm this. The tradition was deep-rooted in the Turko-Mongol areas and continued in parts of Afghanistan, well into the 18th century. Studies prove that camel and carriage-mounted artillery, designed for swift deployment and movement, constituted an important element of Ahmad Shah Abdali's army, which decimated the Marathas in the Third Battle of Panipat in 1761. Here a short description of Babur's military method will not be out of place. Sources continuously refer to his use of Ottoman methods [Chandra, 1999; Briggs, 1966; Price, 1984]. At Panipat, Babur placed his army to the left of the small town, thus protecting his right flank. A large ditch was dug on the left and covered by branches of felled trees (*abatis*) pointing towards the enemy, to prevent the Afghan cavalry from charging upon the left flank. The front itself was arranged according to the Rumi, i.e. Ottoman or Asia Minor fashion. Around 700 carts were strung together with raw hide ropes and between every two carts short breastworks were erected. The matchlock-men stood and discharged their volleys from behind these temporary fortifications in a disciplined manner, in coordination with the artillery. The field cannons were placed in front of the barricades. Babur called this the Rumi method because it had been used to great effect by the Ottoman Turks in a famous battle with Shah Ismail of Iran at Chaldiran in 1514. The arrangement was defensive-offensive and amenable to mobility on the battlefield because the carts could be moved forward as and when required, without breaking the line. To this arrangement Babur added an innovation. In the line of carts, at critical moments during a battle, gaps wide enough for fifty to a hundred horses or men to charge were created at a bow shot apart. "The battle which followed," writes Satish Chandra, "proved to be a triumph of generalship over numbers" [Chandra, 1999: 30].

Babur's main aim, after having chosen the battleground on the advice of his military engineers, and arranged his line, was to break the frontal cavalry attack of the Indo-Afghans. At Panipat, as Farishta writes, "Ibrahim Lodi drew up his forces in one solid mass, and, according to the practice of the Indians, ordered his cavalry to charge. This attack the Mughal army received so steadily, that the Indians began to slacken their pace long before they reached the enemy's line" [Briggs: 29]. The devastating nature of Babur's victory was due to his use of matchlock-men and mixed artillery commanded by thorough professionals. Even before the enemy's cavalry was engaged, his centre was bombarded by field cannons.

Once the concentrated firepower of thousands of matchlocks and scores of artillery pieces threw the under-prepared enemy into confusion, the reserves were sent in to finish the job. While the enemy centre recoiled on itself and the air was rent with the cries of wounded beasts and dying men, the *tulughma* and Babur's advance guard multiplied the damage inflicted by the liberal use of gunpowder. The *tulughma* was a tried Mongol cavalry manoeuvre. This involved wheeling a reserve body of mounted archers round the left and right flanks on the enemy's sides or rear in an attempt to confuse and demoralize it further. Thus the enemy was hemmed in from all sides and most escape routes were sealed. While the enemy flanks caved into its centre, the battle was concluded with the charging units of Babur's household guards, usually with great slaughter. The famous mountain of severed enemy heads followed.

Similar tactics at Khanua yielded similar results. But the remarkable aspect of both battles was their direction and control. Without expert supervision and direction, Babur's plan might have failed. In both battles, the centre was held by Babur who remained close to the artillery at the head of his personal guards. The artillery and matchlock-men, although under capable gunners, were personally supervised by him. The communication system of the Mongols stood in stark contrast to the confusion which prevailed in the Indian ranks. The Bakshi of the camp, with numerous attendants necessary to convey orders, attended to the person of the king. In this way he could receive the final instructions of Babur, which were then "circulated to the different divisions through the *Tawatchies* and *Yesawuls* [adjutants general and exempts]–the commanding generals being forbidden to quit their posts, on any pretext, or to commence action without express orders to that purpose" [Price: section on Panipat and Khanua]. The significance of battlefield communication can hardly be overestimated considering the fact that the front with its right–centre–left combination was often three layers deep. In addition, the reserves and crack *tulughma* units and rear guards had to be managed. The entire front could easily be spread over a couple of zigzag kilometres with units fighting simultaneously at several places.

This description of the Turkish methods brings us to the second event which concludes *Cuckold*: the decisive battle of Khanua fought between a formidable Rajput-Mewati alliance led by the experienced battle hardened Rana Sanga, and the Mughals led by Babur. Nagarkar is right in telling us that it was firepower which destroyed the Rajputs at Khanua. Both Panipat (April 20, 1526) and Khanua (March 16, 1527) established the superiority of artillery and musketry over war-elephants and cavalry. At Panipat, the inexperienced Ibrahim Lodi, according to Babur's estimate, brought almost a thousand war-elephants to crush the Mughals but the Afghans failed to breach Babur's defences. Earlier, as Nagarkar and other scholars assert, Rana Sanga had been in touch with Babur while he was the resident ruler of Kabul, a fact corroborated by Babur himself. If Sanga had diplomatic contacts with Babur and had actually invited him to India to get rid of Ibrahim Lodi, what prevented him from closely examining Mughal military methods? In the year between Panipat and Khanua, the Rajputs made no effort to study the battle in which the Delhi Sultanate perished. According to Rajput calculations, Babur was supposed to return to Kabul after defeating Ibrahim Lodi and plundering Delhi but the Mughals decided to stay and replace the Afghans.

Why did the Rajputs not examine the causes of the Lodi defeat at Panipat? Did this happen because the Rajputs placed their faith in astrology or a minor engagement made them careless? A few days before the decisive Battle of Khanua, the Rajputs had wrested the fort of Bayana from the Mughals telling Babur that the Mughals were not invincible. This, and the size of their army, probably made them over-confident. It is important to remember that on the eve of this battle, Babur disregarded the demoralizing predictions of Muhammad Sharif, an astrologer who had come all the way from Kabul with some reinforcements. The unexpected loss of Bayana coupled with Sharif's depressing predictions seemed to have precipitated a serious crisis in the Mughal ranks. How Babur became a *ghazi* to overcome this is too well known to be repeated here. Sources mention that, after the battle, Sharif gained from Babur's generosity but was also reprimanded.

Had Babur surrendered to astrological predictions, the fate of India might have been different.

The Mughal victories at Panipat and Khanua were spectacular achievements. However, to jump to conclusions on the basis of these victories would be incorrect. The Mughals could hardly have been considered invincible, and moreover, Babur represented a social system which was similar to that of the feudal Rajputs. It is true, however, that Babur was a remarkable man in many ways. As a man of letters, professional soldier and general, he was far superior to the military leaders of the Rajputs and the Indo-Afghans. The world from which he derived knowledge and historical lessons was much larger than the one in which men like Rana Sanga were constrained. However individual brilliance should not be considered as a substitute for systematic change. In history, the role of the individual must be recognized; but individuals are rarely in a position to transform societies through a few well-fought battles. Babur can be called innovative and successful to the extent that he understood the role of gunpowder in 16th century warfare. Rana Sanga was much older than Babur and militarily quite experienced, but his mental attitudes and circumscribed area of operation limited his understanding of warfare.

Given these facts can we imagine a different Battle of Khanua? At Khanua the *tulughma* could have been neutralized by archers drawn in protective rows on the flanks of the main army. A reserve numbering a few thousand cavalry could have been kept outside the range of Babur's cannons to be used in counter-*tulughma* operations on the lines suggested by Nagarkar. The dashing Hasan Khan Mewati or Medini Rai of Chanderi could have handled this. The battle could have been less haphazardly directed without exposing the supreme commander to enemy fire. In fact, a suggestion to this effect made by the Maharaj Kumar in *Cuckold*–that Rana Sanga be placed on a fifty-feet-high mobile tower outside the range of Babur's guns–was shot down by the treacherous Silhadi Rai at the last moment. Ultimately, a contingency plan of orderly retreat could have been put in place to prevent the defeat from becoming a rout. In the event, these possibilities were eliminated by a method predicated upon an excessive reliance on elephants and cavalry.[5] Why did the Rajputs not attack Babur with the aid of a flying column while he was shifting his camp from Sikri to Khanua will remain a mystery forever. Ultimately, Khanua proves that it was Babur who exploited the enemy's weaknesses to greater advantage than Rana Sanga. That is the stuff military victories are made of.

The Battles of Tarain, Panipat, I mean the first and third battles and Khanua, raise the issue of a distinct "Muslim" strategy vis a vis a "Hindu" strategy. Some people suggest that the invading armies triumphed in India because of the internal divisions prevalent in the Hindu armies. There may be some truth in this. However, whether the core of Babur's army was cohesive because it was Muslim or tribal is a question which cannot be answered here.[6] If Islam was a unifying force, Ibrahim Lodi's army should have displayed better cohesion at Panipat. Social cohesion, however, is only one part of the story: technology, tactical methods and leadership all mattered. I do not wish to discuss the communalization of Indian military history here. For our purpose it will be sufficient, and intellectually more productive, to highlight the differences between the Central Asian methods of war and the traditions existing in the subcontinent. In contrast to the Indians who depended on numbers to overwhelm the smaller armies of the northern invaders, the poorer Central Asians and Afghans were swift adventurers par excellence. The Ghaznavids and Ghurids had to depend on light equipment, smaller contingents and speed, given the distance they had travelled from their power base. This seemed imperative because the invaders could never be certain of obtaining sustained local support in India. Hence operational mobility and the ability to concentrate forces at the right conjuncture of time and place made these raiders successful. Nobody can imagine that the Turks could have penetrated India with large unwieldy armies. In the first place, their revenues could never sustain large standing armies, and secondly, these armies would have created insurmountable logistical problems for their commanders. The Turks and Mongols had neither the time nor the resources to waste. In general, they sought brief decisive encounters and, hence, when the mammoth Lodi army showed no signs of activity in Panipat for a while, Babur needled it into action for his own benefit. The Central Asians were not prepared for attrition in potentially hostile territory. Babur's descendants, however, who became completely Indianized in the 17th and 18th centuries, failed to learn the relevant lessons from his strategies, thereby paying a heavy price to adventurers like Nadir Shah and his pupil Ahmad Shah Abdali and also the mobile Marathas. But before that happened his son and heir Humayun was driven into exile by the brilliant Afghan general Farid Khan later known as Sher Shah Suri. Farid had obviously educated himself quite well as a soldier in Babur's army.

In Europe, in the 16th and 17th centuries, near continuous warfare produced a "military revolution." The armies became larger; and the state structure raising and maintaining these armies became increasingly institutionalized and complex. Artillery, infantry and navies developed new forms and adapted themselves to technological progress. However, viewed in a trans-historical perspective, the development of military organization, order, form, strategy and technology were not exclusive to Europe. There were other areas where the impact of war on society led to lasting changes in social formations. The importance of these changes appears even more striking compared with the military equilibrium achieved by the warring states of feudal India. In Indian history, from the exploits of Chandragupta Maurya and the south Indian Cholas to the tripartite struggle for Kanauj, there is no shortage of warfare. But let us briefly examine what happened in ancient China.

In Chinese history, the period between 770 and 221 BC is known as the "Warring States Era." Out of this era grew the massive armies of up to one million, belonging to the large states. Significant tactical changes also occurred simultaneously. Aristocratic charioteers armed with bows gradually gave way to massed conscript infantry, armed with spears and iron swords. By 221 BC, the Chinese "military revolution" had been accomplished and a system had been created in China which endured, with minimal change, for almost two millennia. The Great Wall of China and the enormous mausoleum of Prince Cheng, larger than the pyramids, guarded by an army of 6,000 life-size terracotta figures, belong to this period. These figures narrate a tale of the amazing efficiency and centralization achieved by China in the 3rd century BC. These statues are shown wearing standardized uniforms with colour-coded insignia denoting their units. In comparison, the regimental system in India was finally created by the British. While China stands out as an example of military innovation, countries like Vietnam are not far behind. The successful Vietnamese first fought against the Japanese, then the French and finally the United States, during the 1940s, 50s, 60s and 70s. Their eventual victory was predicated upon the Vietcong's ability to learn the correct lessons from history and apply unorthodox military methods in the execution of a people's war. In their overall understanding of war, the Chinese and Vietnamese have generally been ahead of others, and many of their effective strategic traditions are, in fact, quite old.[7] Not to fight on the enemy's terms or by enemy standards is ingrained in Far Eastern strategic thought. To innovatively recreate traditions has been their strength.

With this as a background, it becomes useful to ask how many units of Mewar we remember. Why is it that the warrior Rajputs, the favourite "martial race" of the British, never produced a proper treatise on warfare? However, they were not alone in Indian history in their peculiar attitude towards war, much of which was characterized by the *kesari bana* and *jauhar*–both glorified by Bollywood but essentially wasteful activities. Regarding artillery, except a Tipu here or a Ranjit Singh there, the rest of India seemed to share the Rajput view. Even the Marathas who had emerged as the foremost military power of 17th and 18th century India, relied far too much on cavalry and hand-to-hand combat with sword and shield. At Panipat, in 1761, they depended on the artillery park of the French trained adventurer Ibrahim Khan 'Gardi'. It was their ignorance of the "mechanics of retreat" which led to their disorderly flight from Panipat in 1761. When confronting the Afghans, they departed from their guerrilla tactics without understanding the modalities of modern war, and paid a heavy price for their ignorance. After the Panipat debacle the Maratha Sardars began to modernize their infantry and artillery with the help of European expertise but this did not prevent their defeat at the hands of the English East India Company in the Second Anglo Maratha War (1803-05).

Had *Cuckold* been available at the court of Rana Sanga, it would have become great source material for strategic warfare. It is, however, a modern novel, a complex mix of history and fiction. This essay has glanced at some of the military questions raised by it, but has deliberately provided only one reading of the novel. *Cuckold* cannot, however, be reduced to just the treatment of military matters. There is much more to it for historians who study the social, economic and political complexities of everyday life. In sum, novels like *Cuckold* are invaluable for changing popular perceptions of history. By locating the military problematic in the complex of systems, mentalities and technology, Nagarkar reminded us of the comparative nature of history. War appears as a window to state formations in this paradigm and we come to realize that the causes of victory and defeat are not only to be found on the dusty battlefields of military history but in the mentalities of the warriors who produce those battlefields.

NOTES

1. Based on a paper presented at a seminar on Kiran Nagarkar's Fiction organized by the English Department of the University of Mumbai on March 7, 2001. A revised version was presented at the NMMI, Teen Murti on September 4, 2001.
2. I prefer to call this the *chaturanga* or chessboard method of Hindu warfare. It rarely worked in the face of professional invading armies. The 'standing armies' of ancient Indian kingdoms were not professional in the strict sense of the term. They were rarely divorced from society and had no system of common messing, professional training or systematic

deployment on long campaigns. They lacked the *esprit de corps* which characterized some of the veteran Roman Legions.

3. Sources clearly suggest that the Rajput kingdoms of north and north-western India were perpetually at war with each other during the medieval period. Some of these kingdoms had, in fact, emerged from the Tripartite Struggle for Kannauj preceding the Ghazanavid and Ghurid invasions of the medieval period. By the early 16th century, when Mewar was almost continuously at war with Gujarat and Malwa, the Rajputs had already acquired a martial reputation largely due to the labours of men like Rana Kumbha and his descendant Rana Sanga. Much of this reputation remained intact during the Mughal period when the Rajputs served in extraordinarily large numbers in the Mughal armies. Later, the British reinforced the self-image of the Rajputs by classifying them as a first rate "martial race" and recruited them heavily into the Indian army. The martial self-image of the Rajputs is, therefore, not merely a product of British colonial needs and classification. The image is as much historical as discursive, and was sustained by the status of the Rajputs as the ruling elite of Rajputana.
4. Al-Biruni, *India*. New Delhi: NBT. 1993, 10-11, Biruni calls the Hindus "haughty, foolishly vain, self-conceited, and stolid." Furthermore the learned Hindus refused to acknowledge the advances made in scientific matters in Persia or Khorasan. The Hindus did not travel much for fear of becoming impure and hence did not learn much from societies placed outside the subcontinent.
5. The Rajput reliance on these animals should be understood in context. The elephant was kept for ceremonial purposes, to execute opponents and criminals, and to enhance imperial prestige. The horse gave the tribute and revenue collecting elite much needed mobility. The sword and lance-wielding Rajput *sawar* was militarily superior to the cultivator in every possible way. The socio-economic conditions of medieval India did not produce the historical need for much military innovation. In such circumstances the military accent remained on numbers, and hand-to-hand combat in the last resort.

6. The cohesion of Babur's army seemed to have broken down on the eve of the Battle of Khanua. Only his exceptional qualities, a political appeal to Islam, and disregard for astrology saved the day for the Mughals.
7. During the anti-colonial wars of the 20th century, the Chinese and Vietnamese people led by the Communist Parties successfully adapted traditional methods of conducting protracted war to suit contemporary needs. Tradition was not blindly followed, but creatively reconstructed in a period when China and Vietnam were passing through a phase of total war. This creativity underpinned the success of the Chinese against the Japanese and the Chang Kai Shek led Kuomintang during and after the Second World War. The Vietnamese were successful first against the French colonialists and later against the technological might of the United States.

REFERENCES

Satish Chandra, *Medieval India: From Sultanat to the Mughals, 1206-1526*. New Delhi: Har-Anand, 1997.

____, *Medieval India From Sultanat to the Mughals, Volume II, 1526-1748*. New Delhi: Har-Anand, 1999.

Carl von Clausewitz, *On War*. Princeton: Princeton University Press, 1984.

Kasim Mahomed Ferishta, *History of the Rise of the Mahomedan Power in India Till the Year A.D. 1612*. Trans. John Briggs. Vol. 2. Calcutta, 1966.

Geoffrey Parker, *The Military Revolution: Military Innovation and the Rise of the West, 1500-1800*. Cambridge: Cambridge University Press, 1988.

Ishwari Prasad, *The Mughal Empire*. Allahabad: Chugh Publications, 1974.

Major David Price (ed.), *Mahommedan History from the Death of the Arabian Legislator to the Accession of the Emperor Akbar and the Establishment of the Moghul Empire in Hindustan–from Original Persian Authorities,Volume III, Part II*. 1821. New Delhi: Inter-India Publications, 1984.

Stephen Peter Rosen, *Societies and Military Power: India and its Armies.* New Delhi: Oxford University Press, 1996.

Russell Stetler (ed.), *The Military Art of People's War: Selected Writings of General Vo Nguyen Giap.* London: Monthly Review Press, 1971.

S.N. Sen, *The Military System of the Marathas.* 1928. Calcutta: K.P. Bagchi & Co., 1979.

5

War and Cinema[1]

> Narrative too is a form the historian shares with the creative writer–and it explains much of the appeal that history has traditionally enjoyed with the reading public. Like other forms of story-telling, historical narrative can entertain through its ability to create suspense and arouse powerful emotions. But narrative is also the historian's basic technique for conveying what it felt like to observe or participate in past events.
>
> –John Tosh, *The Pursuit of History*, p. 125.

Photography and cinematography are 19th century inventions which revolutionized the imagination of history. They made personal and social histories possible and realistic in many ways. Almost everything was photographed from the 1830s and the camera produced the breed of professional photographers which has thrived since then. As the photographic archive began to grow in America and Europe among the events which attracted professional and amateur photographers most were wars and calamities like earthquakes and famines. The first major wars to be extensively photographed were the Crimean War (1853-56) and the American Civil War (1861-65). The photographic evidence produced by these wars was used extensively by the print media of the times. The combination of the reports filed by war correspondents and photos sent from the battlefields, camps, marches, trenches and military hospitals created a new awareness of war among the public across the world. When the public demanded more photographic evidence of world events photographers began travelling to the colonies in increased numbers. Events like the Revolt of 1857 in India or the frequent famines caused by colonial policies became hot topics for European photographers. The metropolitan imagery of the tropics was enriched by the recreation of the colonies in the photographs. Wildlife and nature photography developed alongside what we might call photographic anthropology which often helped shape public discourses on the idea of civilization. The transition from a photo archive and studio to an archive of cinematography was made in the late 19th century. From then onwards film, as history and historical source, began to grip the public imagination across the world. In these circumstances it is not surprising to note that the First World War (1914-18), the Spanish Civil War (1936-39) and the Second World War (1939-45) yielded a huge cinema archive which historians continue to use till date. More, and hitherto unpublicized, photographs and films of these and other noteworthy events of the 20th century keep surfacing on the media from time to time enriching our knowledge of the follies committed by our forefathers. At the same time from the early 20th century the cinematograph (movie camera) helped produce artefacts of modern ideology known as the feature film and documentary. Studios, outdoor shoots, costumes, sound, professional film actors, cinema halls and a film going public comprised an influential event increasingly from the early 20th century. The trendsetters of cinema like D.W. Griffith did not waste time converting their medium into an ideological message for their viewers. The three-hour long controversial *The Birth of a Nation* (1915) presented a mix of film aesthetics, racism and white nationalism to American audiences and became a model for nation films made elsewhere.

Periodically war films receive awards and top the popularity charts. What can explain the popularity of war films and the longevity of the war-film genre? What sustains public interest in war and its filming either as feature or documentary? The answer to these questions can be sought in the relationship of war, memory and modern national and cultural existence. Contemporary and historical war and associated patriotic sacrifice is central to the imagination of the nation. Almost all nation-states are modern and draw upon military memories to sustain themselves ideologically and materially. Nationalism and war are usually combined in the mainstream war movie but the corpus of films criticizing war, and thereby undermining nationalism, is also quite large. The Indian contribution to the genre of realistic and critical war-films is negligible and the reasons for this are mentioned in this chapter. War has always been central to nationalist mythology. The Marxist military historian Arthur Marwick outlines the context of the relationship between war and nationalism in the following words:

> Wars loom large in the memories of ordinary human beings; particularly this is true of those who have directly encountered the intense excitement, as well as the dreadful tragedy and suffering, of war, who have been projected by war into new jobs, new experiences, and perhaps, a new sense of purpose and self-esteem, or who have been swayed by the claims both of government propagandists and idealistic activists that the horror and sacrifice of war must necessarily lead to the creation of a better world. Even if those personally involved in the second of the twentieth century's total wars are now passing from the scene, *younger generations still absorb national myths, mainly through television and simplified textbooks and they still feel the perennial fascination exerted by tales of human slaughter on a massive scale.*[2] [emphasis added]

Before commenting on some Indian war films a few remarks on Hindi cinema's treatment of war and the military in general will not be out of place. Needless to add that this treatment ought to be viewed in relation to memory, myth and ideas of masculine nationhood mentioned in the large body of literature on the subject. The acclaimed works of Benedict Anderson and Eric Hobsbawm have established beyond reasonable doubt that the nation comprises an imagined community stitched together by print capitalism and political ideologies. Nationalism is a political project of every society's vested interests. Mythical nationalist history and its cinematic form are essential parts of the nation's attempt to recreate itself continuously and seek popular sanction. Antonio Gramsci described this process as hegemony. The chief beneficiaries of this process can easily be identified and labelled either the military-industrial complex or the politico-military complex. Minor beneficiaries include the service professionals and intellectuals involved in the business of producing nation films. Tagore once famously wrote that nationalism in the ultimate analysis is the creed of the mob and hooligans. The importance attached to battles and military history by the monumental Hindustani historical film is a direct outcome of the dominant historiography and ideology which guided filmmaking in India. Since nationalism is widely projected and accepted essentially as a masculine and patriarchal discourse war comes naturally to it. Nothing like a war to stimulate the nationalist hormones! However, the importance accorded to war by commercial Hindi cinema has been one-sided. Analysing, and learning from defeat, has never been a particularly strong characteristic of Indian war portrayals. A salient feature of Hindi cinema's enduring relationship with the armed forces and war is their use as props for romantic and nationalist themes. Hence, this cinema has neither conceptually problematized the armed forces nor their involvement in war in general. Following this, the question of critically and sensitively dealing with the dialectics of society and war has so far not seriously been raised by Indian commercial cinema. Further, the war film has been conveniently used to legitimize and promote Hindu religious and patriarchal values and widely held superstitions which are common to commercial Indian cinema of all kinds. The Indian war film, like its mainstream commercial counterpart, is geared to an audience which is intensely jingoistic and, to use Satyajit Ray's words, backward and unsophisticated. In fact, it can be asserted that by shying away from criticizing war and the armed forces Hindi cinema has become complicit with Indian, and increasingly Hindu, nationalism. In a country where masses of people are easily driven into fits of madness by their belief in myths, making films critical of the nation's military and history is practically impossible. In societies ruled by mobs led by political demagogues or religious leaders critical cinema becomes "parallel" cinema or even niche cinema meant for and appreciated by an insecure group of intelligent people.

The commercial and popular Hindi films which feature the military portray the armed forces as deeply masculine, straight, nationalist, self-sacrificing and ideal. Of late a number of films have extended this liberality to the police glorifying guns, violence and even custodial torture. Many of these *Shool*, *Dabang* and *Singham* type films are cathartic in their psychological orientation. They provide visual compensation and the satisfaction of revenge to the audience which, in reality, is helpless against the nexus of crime, capital and politics. All this is in keeping with the dominant media image of these state forces. TV crime programmes involving the police try their best to promote the wrong belief that the police are apolitical. The definitions and selection of crimes by the producers of these programmes like the long running and extremely crude *CID* on a privately owned TV channel have a clear bias in favour of murder investigations. Financial crime has blighted India's prospects in the times of globalization but crime-based programmes like Crime Patrol never focus on financial crime or crimes committed by politicians. Given the holy cow status enjoyed by the Indian armed forces in India, Bollywood producers have never gathered courage to criticize them on or off screen. I only remember one film called *Shaurya*, based on the communal response of a senior Army officer to the Kashmir insurgency, which deconstructs the influence of communalism on senior army officers. The film redeems two honest soldiers of the Army one of whom is sent by the Army to investigate the case. The guilty officer is finally court martialled and the professionalism of the Indian Army upheld. Otherwise the Bollywood war film connects the mainstream and margins of Indian society like its other commercial cousins. It has never occurred to a Bollywood producer that the Indian Army, even if temporarily, is actually viewed as an army of occupation in many disturbed parts of

India. No Indian filmmaker has ever made a film on the people who live in states affected by the draconian Armed Forces Special Powers Act (AFSPA). Have the counter-insurgency operations of the Indian armed forces and paramilitary forces in areas where they exercise impunity under the AFSPA ever been converted into a people-sensitive film? Has any Bollywood producer, including Mani Ratnam of *Roja* fame, ever paid critical attention to the routine civil and human rights violations integral to these counter-insurgency operations carried out in the name patriotism? The answers to these questions is a resolute no because of the weaknesses of Indian civil society mentioned earlier in this book. In a context where the making of war films is coloured by propaganda the question of filming and presenting cinema narratives of blunders in Sri Lanka (1987-89) or Kashmir (1989-2008) or Manipur or on the Indo-Bangladesh border (2002) simply does not arise. This is not to say that propagandist films *per se* are devoid of technical excellence, artistic merit and social content. However, the relationship of propaganda and art is a complex matter which is best left untouched in this essay. While discussing the films and career of the noted and controversial German filmmaker Leni Riefenstahl, who died in 2003, the film critic Indrajit Hazra raises a fundamental and disturbing question: can great art spring from a bad idea?[3] This question is also applicable to the music of Richard Wagner usually known as a racialist composer greatly appreciated by Hitler and the Nazis. Wagner's son-in-law, the Kaiser's social anthropologist and Hitler's 'John the Baptist', was the rabid anti-Semite social Darwinist, Houston Stewart Chamberlain. Of all things, Wagner was called "an unquestionable genius of the theatre and music" by non other than Edward Said (Le Monde *diplomatique*, October 2001). Riefenstahl is known for her Nazi era films like the *Triumph of the Will* (1934), a powerful documentary made in the service of Hitler. The film is known for creating a visual effect through a sea of Nazi salutes and imposing swastika banners fluttering in the German breeze. Also known is her *Olympia* (1938) an ode to the visual pleasure of the human form based on the 1936 Berlin Olympics, a showcase event of the Nazi regime.

However, her focus on the athletic Jessie Owens infuriated Hitler who had wanted his favourite 'Aryan' athlete to defeat Owens. The works of Wagner and Riefenstahl raise a fundamental question of art: is moral correctness a prerequisite for the making of great art? Do political correctness and good art necessarily go together? If not, it must take exceptional courage and probity on the part of a critic to differentiate between ideology and art. The art of political incorrectness can also be praised and admired even as the artist's ideological leanings are questioned and debated.

The immaculate armed forces have been used as an exciting adventurous background against which innumerable bourgeois love stories have been picturized by Hindi cinema. Occasionally they have provided spice to the bland staple of middle-class or *faux* rural song and dance rubbish dished out by Bollywood year after year. Most of Indian stardom which is politically opportunist emanates from this cinematic opiate to which the mob is addicted. Tele-serials are poor copies of such films and run for months on channels reinforcing sexual and cultural stereotypes. I sometimes like to call this the Mills and Boons Syndrome of Bollywood. Let us see how the military uniform has appeared in Hindi cinema. From *Hum Dono* featuring Dev Anand in a double role in the 1950s to Raj Kapoor's triangular love story *Sangam* of the 1960s through to *Aradhana* of Rajesh Khanna fame of the early 1970s, uniforms have been worn by Indian stars to buttress socially entrenched tropes of love, fidelity, national service, honour and, above all, correct projections of masculinity. Films like *Prem Pujari* and *Hindustan Ki Kasam* were Bollywood tributes to the Indian military. A feature worth noticing in these films is the petty bourgeois character of the military hero who is invariably shown as a young, though mature, boyish, middle-level officer. This blends perfectly with other projections of exclusivist bourgeois nationhood in Hindi cinema. This particular aspect of such films is also heavily underscored by the so-called army officer culture depicted in various scenes and episodes; the 'ballroom' and party sequences often involving romantic songs with pianos thrown in, caricatured Anglicization of senior officers sporting handle bar moustaches, the bars and drinking bouts, the vehicles such as the macho jeeps driven by the heroes often quite recklessly and the tragic deaths of heroes in accidents or action, etc. Going by the fairy tales woven by Hindi movies, military officers are supposed to make good romantic husbands found irresistible by beautiful, and fiercely loyal, Indian women who are throwbacks to the *adarsh naris* or *patnis* promoted by Indian print journalism since the 19th century. In *Aradhana* this fidelity remains unbreached even after the young Air Force officer's death in an accident. There is no need for chastity belts in such normative descriptions of military social life. This could not have been otherwise because in Hindi films till at least the late 1970s widow remarriage happens, in any case, very rarely. The widow is usually cast as someone inauspicious. It is worth remembering that widows, with their special social and sexual handicaps, also constitute an important margin of Hindi cinema[4].

The problem of defining genres continues with the treatment of Hindi war movies. Are Hindi cinema's military ventures essentially love stories? Quite often they succeed in weaving love and political statements together. Take the case of Manoj Kumar's *Upkaar* which was made almost immediately after the Indo-Pak war of 1965. This propaganda hit was an unabashed tribute to Lal Bahadur Shastri's slogan *Jai Jawan, Jai Kisan*. The making of the film was also influenced by the famine-like conditions and other shortages prevalent in the country during the second half of the 1960s. At least one song in the movie alludes to the social ills responsible for and produced by these shortages and the black market spawned by them in the country. In *Upkaar* the hero is the archetype north Indian middle peasant who dons the army uniform when the nation needs him as a soldier; *the kisan becomes the jawan*. An old peasant in uniform story. While he is away on the front fighting the Pakistanis and shouting *Bharat Mata ki Jai* things go horribly wrong in his village. Greedy, and also largely urban, enemies from within conspire to pollute the culturally pure atmosphere of the village. The victorious *jawan* returns home to set the house in order; both social order and nation triumph in one united moment *Upkaar* tried to drive home the romantic, though entirely misconstrued, point that India lives in its villages and its goodness is essentially rural and land-based. There is a love story in the film too but the overall message of the film, as in other films made by Manoj Kumar, is overtly cultural and political.[4] However, even *Upkaar* cannot be called a war movie. The border war is peripheral to the main theme of the film which is centred on definitions of Indian nationhood and culture which was expanded in *Poorab Aur Paschim* later by Manoj Kumar. In contrast to the three bourgeois war films mentioned earlier, *Upkaar* presents the main protagonist as a rural stereotype. Nonetheless, it could be argued that the peasant-soldier-hero of *Upkaar* is neither a rural Dalit proletarian nor a feudal landlord but a *kisan*–essentially an upper caste peasant proprietor resolutely opposed to the violation, alienation or division of his land, i.e. a metaphor for his mother.[5] Can this *kisan*, who readily becomes the *jawan*, be viewed as the rural counterpart of the public-school-educated urban bourgeois who becomes an officer in the same army? An affirmative answer to this question would mean that *Upkaar* only re-locates the male bourgeois protagonist from an urban to rural setting. All other things, including the gender equations governed by patriarchal norms essential to the nation, remain the same[5].

In contrast to India, a genre of war films does exist in the West. Most of the war films made on the Second World War, for instance, almost certainly belong to this genre. It is not as if these films, like the Indian films which touch upon military subjects, are not propagandist. These films, like the Westerns, are heroic narratives. They offer a heavy dose of monumental history without necessarily locating the historical subject in the ancient or medieval periods. They often have romantic sub plots which reinforce the gender-nation equations of Western societies, but they remain focused on war in general. Military equipment used in these films is authentic and their handling of detail is praiseworthy although the overall portrayal of war in them roughly equals sketches of war contained in the popular adolescent level *Commando* readings. Films like *The Longest Day*, for example, show the 1944 Allied landings in Normandy in significant military detail with adequate coverage given to the reactions of the German General Staff. Soviet films are also good in this respect, although understandably their focus remains on showing the exploits of the Red Army as part of the Great Patriotic war waged against the German invaders. Other films, without being necessarily critical of war *per se*, offer insights which are almost totally missing from Hindi commercial cinema's amateur dabbling in military matters. *The Bridge on the River Kwai*, shot exclusively in Sri Lanka, narrates a heroic tale of individual struggles against wartime Japanese brutality in South-East Asia. It is a narration of events from the Allied viewpoint, but nonetheless exposes the horrors of war in the 20th century. One film which must be mentioned in this context is the splendid German film *Stalingrad* (1993) by Joseph Vilsmaier which provides a worm's eye view of the bloodiest battle in history and drives home the message that death in battle is painful and horrific. The realities of modern industrial war do not square with the image of heroic war used by politicians to delude their followers. War is hell for the soldier and civilian alike.

Other dimensions of war have also been explored by Western filmmakers. Films made in the 1970s included the *Great Escape* which narrates the story of a valiant escape of allied POWs from a German POW camp. On the other hand, *Escape from Sorbibor*, unlike *Schindler's List* discussed below, shows a group of enterprising Jews as agents of history. Here the focus shifts to the victims in a German concentration camp who finally regain freedom by exercising volition. The film is shot from the perspective of the underdog. *Hell in the Pacific* is a sensitive and humanist film about a Japanese soldier and an American serviceman marooned on an island in the Pacific Ocean. These two do not understand each other's languages but this barrier is soon overcome and a friendship based on mutual respect and abilities needed for survival soon develops. Unfortunately, this egalitarian relationship–with its unambiguous message of universal humanism–comes to an end when the two are discovered by their respective sides towards the end of the film. The film delivers a strong critique of the process of othering by placing the military uniform in context.

And who can forget *Schindler's List* by Spielberg, a heroic story turned into an impressive war film? Set in the context of the Second World War and the *Final Solution* executed by the Nazis, and made with resources only Hollywood producers can command, its imagery of the liquidation of Polish Jews by the Nazis could remain unsurpassed for quite some time. The role of Schindler, a German businessman who saved the lives of eleven hundred Polish Jews from the Nazis, was essayed by the brilliant Liam Neeson. So well received was the film in Germany that its screening set off the discovery of many local Schindlers. Recently this film has been criticized for Americanizing the Holocaust with the aid of Hollywood techniques and traditions of making heroic historical.[7] In addition the hand of the American Jewish lobby may be discerned in the making of *Schindler's List*, but even a contemporary critique of the film does not fail to notice that it shows the transformation of an 'opportunist, gambler, and philanderer...into Schindler the heroic rescuer'. In addition, the film does not fail to highlight the horrors of genocide despite undertaking a highly subjective, and even fetishized, portrayal of Jews as victims of German tyranny. This film should be watched with *Shoah*, the longest documentary on the Holocaust made by the French filmmaker Claude Lanzmann. *Shoah* (1985) relies heavily on interviews done over a long period with the witnesses, victims, executors and historians of the holocaust to highlight the apparent professional normalcy of the final solution[6].

War films like *Hamburger Hill, Saving Private Ryan*, the *Apocalypse Now*, *Deer Hunter, Platoon* and *Full Metal Jacket* must also be mentioned in this context for their extremely sensitive portrayal of 20th-century warfare and the catastrophic US defeat in the Vietnam military quagmire. The alternative interpretations of war, and popular participation in it, offered by these films is worth examining in the context of visual representations of history in general. The *Deer Hunter* must be mentioned as a powerful, sensitive and realistic Vietnam film which focuses on the transformation in a US conscript's character (played by the incomparable Robert De Niro) as he moves in and out of the military uniform. This is not a regular story of a boy ending up as a man in a combat-hardened army, but that of the transformation wrought in an individual by his participation in war. In the last scene he lowers his hunting rifle and lets the deer escape, whereas the film begins with a deer hunt and the masculine revelry associated with it. In between are visits to a futile, dehumanizing and maddening war. These films should be remembered for portraying war as it really is–political, inhuman, wasteful and gory despite the fact that some may be accused of showing war from the US perspective. Nonetheless, this is war shorn of its masculine imagery, mythological glory and 'embedded' reportage. War has also been shot as a discovery of counter narrative literally from the other side with a distinct subaltern perspective; Kevin Costner's brilliant portrayal of the unjust Indian wars in *Dances With Wolves* comes to mind here and so does the criticism it received at the hands of white Americans. Costner's visual deconstruction of the otherwise heavily ideological genre of Westerns will long be remembered by film buffs and critics alike. *Dances With Wolves* relates to a chapter of genocide in US history and the power of its Anglo-Saxon elite as very few films have done. Towards the end of the film, Costner's protagonist (a white soldier of the US Army played by Costner himself), fondly called *Dances With Wolves* by the Native Americans, is left with no choice but to join them as a rebel deserter from the US Army. The political and historical implications of such an unconventional end are quite clear; the film is a successful inversion of the Western genre which is normally dedicated to glorifying the White nationalist history of the United States. What makes such films possible is a civil society which creates space for dissent. The Vietnam war and the draft was imposed on US citizens by a cold war state indebted to the military industrial complex. The consequence was a massive anti-war movement in the country which created room for critical filmmaking of the disaster in the 1970s and 80s.

Compared with films like the *Deer Hunter* and *Saving Private Ryan* the scope of Bollywood war films is restricted to showcasing official propaganda and jingoism. Hence, no Bombay producer has dared to produce a film on the rich and unfortunate experiences of the Indian Army in Sri Lanka between 1987 and 1989. No oral or visual history of these wars from the viewpoint of Indian privates who died unsung is available to the Indian people. I also do not remember a documentary being made on the policy blunders in Sri Lanka. How instructive such ventures might be in the context of official contemplations of deploying Indian troops as stabilizers or peace-keepers in other parts of the world can well be imagined. How can Bollywood's neglect of such crucial military matters be explained? Could this have happened because an ultra-conservative Indian Censor Board, cast in the Victorian-Colonial mould would never have cleared a war film critical of official versions? Or this did not happen because Bollywood considers itself nationalist enough not to attempt even a mild criticism of India's border war and other activities of the Indian armed forces? I think most Indian film producers are too terrified of the state to approach military matters critically. These conditions are, however, not applicable to potential themes set in the colonial period. Nonetheless, Bollywood producers have never tried to capitalize on the real historical experience of Indian troops in Mesopotamia, Africa or India's north-east and Burma for reasons best known to them. The self-censorship of Bollywood, as far as historical war films is concerned, is evident and worth probing.

Let us focus on *Haqeeqat* (Reality), perhaps the best war film produced by Bollywood. An accurate, though brief, entry in the *Encylopaedia of Indian Cinema* describes this film as a 'propaganda film dedicated to Nehru and trading on the resurgence of nationalist sentiment in the wake of the India-China war of 1962 which provides the film's setting'[7]. The *Encyclopaedia* also makes a note of the rhetorical highlights of the film and the mixing of documentary shots of Nehru and Zhou En-Lai with the main nationalist narrative. Another source describes *Haqeeqat* as a 'leftist' film 'with the message of nationalist propaganda about an incident during the Indo-China war–how an Indian patrol is more or less wiped out in a mountain battle.' The film, however, 'deals honestly with the mistakes made by the leaders and the defeat suffered by India in the war.'[8] These are two entirely different descriptions. The following suggests that these brief descriptions are not enough and much more needs to be said about the film. *Haqeeqat* was perhaps the first genuine war movie made after Indian independence and most probably laid down the guidelines for Indian war films which followed. Its relationship with Indian nationalism and the post-colonial Indian state needs to be unpacked to place it in the context of historicals outlined in the preceding pages. Towards this end, *Haqeeqat* is being deconstructed below with reference to two main aspects of the film. First, the portrayal of the Indian Army and the place of war in the historical rhetoric of Indian nationalism. Second, the love theme/plot and its ideological correlation with nation and territory.

Something had to be done for the Indian Army by the Bombay film industry in the aftermath of the devastating Indo-China war of 1962. The war had been a disaster for India on all fronts. The prestige of the professional Indian Army, comprising the so-called martial races of India and an officer corps constituted and working on the British pattern, was significantly lowered, if not altogether shattered, by the resounding victory of the People's Liberation Army of China. The behaviour of many important Indian Army officers during the war left the Army in a state of crisis once the brief war ended. The manner in which the war began and ended showed that the initiative in the whole affair remained firmly in Chinese hands. On the whole the war, which exposed the nascent Indian Republic's military and strategic weaknesses, dealt a body blow to Indian military pride, civilian morale and Nehruvian foreign policy idealism. To the Indian nationalist the debacle of 1962 came as a rude wake-up call. It was also seen as an indictment of Nehru's increasingly unrealistic-appearing policies designed to promote Third World peace and cooperation by a growing band of Nehru's critics in India. In the event the Chinese attack became a convenient stick to beat India's first and, increasingly helpless, Prime Minister. Following the war, Nehru and his advisors were subjected to intense and endless criticism by the political Right in India–a trend which has continued till date. In such circumstances, a film rescuing the honour of the Indian Army, and thereby allaying increasing social insecurities, was desperately needed to revive country-wide morale. In the months after the war, not only was Nehru in a crisis but the entire vision of Indian nationalism which his personality symbolized stood undermined.

Hence, it is easy to see why *Haqeeqat* zoomed in on Ladakh where the condition of the Indian Army was not as bad as it was in the NEFA (North-East Frontier Agency). The NEFA, now the state of Arunachal Pradesh, is claimed by China even today. The film is centred on platoon level defensive actions which in themselves could not have been too significant to the outcome of war in the Aksai Chin region. Throughout the film the heavily outnumbered Indians are shown desperately defending border posts (*chowkies*) against sloppy Chinese attacks. However, one of the advantages of narrating platoon- or company-level action lies in the display of camaraderie. This is also resorted to in casual conversation laced with bravado between the defenders even as the Chinese advance, to be shot as sitting ducks, in overwhelming numbers. A platoon or company can easily become a brotherly nation in microcosm pitted against the faceless 'other'. Towards this end *Haqeeqat* is more or less successful, although the social composition of the platoon in question appears more north-Indian than pan-Indian.[11] This becomes clear from the conversations which the *jawans* hold amongst themselves and the memories they re-live and share before being killed by the Chinese in action. The domestic scenes conveyed in flashback during the *jawans*' narrations portray a contented north Indian peasantry possessed of beautiful women, adequate means of production, military traditions and a relaxed life. Some of these scenes were shot in studios carefully designed to fit widespread urban perceptions of rural India in those days. These are not soldiers made by economic need as such but by Rajput or Jat pride in military service; portraying the *jawans* in this way tends to mitigate the class rivalries which might have otherwise surfaced during a military debacle like the one faced by the Indian army in 1962[9]. The makers of *Haqeeqat* overlooked the fact that an army in retreat can often become a seething mass of disaffection; this would have militated against the goal of national-social unity to which the film was dedicated.

The positive part of *Haqeeqat's* imagery, mediated though the hardships of the *jawans* and officers and scenes from their private lives, can be seen in its apparent secularism. To be fair to the filmmakers, it must be said that the film is not aimed against a religious community; this religious slant is more obvious in films like *Upkaar* and *Border*. But the following must also be observed. The absence of religious bias in the film can be explained in two ways. First, the film was made by 'former Marxists' who, I take the liberty of presuming, could become nationalist on occasion but rarely communal. Second, the enemy in the film is China and not Pakistan; therefore, thematically the question of religion entering the othering of the opponent does not arise. However, this precisely gave the opportunity to the filmmakers to showcase a united effort of all Indians to meet the Chinese challenge. This opportunity to define Indian nationalism in inclusive terms is lost because the communities, individuals, symbols and metaphors used in the film to drive home messages of India's nation-form are entirely Hindu and north Indian. Leave alone pan-religious, they are not even pan-Indian. Not a single noteworthy military character in the film is either a Muslim, Sikh or Christian. Nor is he Bengali, Tamil, Assamese, Kashmiri, etc., for that matter. In eclipsing these religious and regional margins the film conforms to the model of media representation sketched in earlier parts of this study. For instance, in at least two scenes depicting the demoralization of defeated *jawans* and attempts by their officers to rouse them to action recourse to specific Hindu symbols is taken. In one scene a *jawan* proudly proclaims his Rajput lineage while lamenting retreat being preferred to death on the battlefield. He is reassured by the officer in charge who emphasizes the importance of tactical retreat. In another scene Balraj Sahni (the Major) exhorts his men to move with a reference to the coming festival of lights, Diwali. This has clear Hindu martial overtones because Diwali stands for the successful return of the victorious Shri Ram to Ayodhya from the great battlefield in Sri Lanka. This equates the Indians with Ram and the Chinese with Ravana–a metaphor reinforced by the final song *Kar chale hum fidaa jaano tan sathiyon*. A stanza (in which the scene of the heroine's clothes being ripped off by the Chinese is replayed to reinforce the message) in the song clearly says the following:

Khench do apne khoon se zameen par lakeer,
Is taraf aane paaye naa Ravana koi,
Tod do haath agar haath uthne lage,
Choone paye naa Sita ka daaman koi,
Ram bhi tum, tumhi Laxman saathiyo . . .

The closest the film comes to essentializing the Chinese as one of the several northern invaders who periodically invaded India is to be found in a scene where the Major in command (the fair and handsome six feet two inches tall Balraj Sahni) inspires his *jawans* to fight the Chinese. In a long melodramatic monologue, Sahni is shown defending the Indian position on the border dispute with China. He reiterates the myth that Indians have never been invaders and the Chinese are doing what invaders down from Alexander, Changez Khan and Timur have always done to India. This nationalist myth presupposes the historical existence of territorial India as we know it today. Sahni's melodramatic speech and gestures involve the excoriating of Mao's *Red Book* which is finally bayonetted by a *jawan* roused to fury by Sahni's speech. In another scene two soldiers are shown exchanging racist remarks about the Chinese. Sahni's harangue is predicated upon well-established nationalist notions of Indian unity, and even racial superiority, since antiquity in opposition to external forces bent upon destroying India's national and territorial integrity. The interesting part in this scene is the point of Sahni's entry into the *jawans*' underground bunker. The *jawans* are in the middle of a heated discussion on the seemingly pointless border dispute the outcome of which, discerning views might observe, could lead to the growth of rational thinking among them to the detriment of territorial nationalist claims in both contending sides. At this crucial juncture nationalist ideology is injected into the scene in the form of a history lesson delivered by an educated middle-class commissioned officer of the rank of Major. This deflects the danger of demoralization and consequent disorder in the ranks and the *jawans* are temporarily swept up by the nationalist rhetoric. It is not surprising that the film does not mention that India's insistence on asserting the MacMohan line drawn by the British imperialists between Tibet and India might also have contributed to the worsening of the Sino-Indian border dispute.

On the whole, *Haqeeqat* tries to redeem the Indian Army by portraying it as a community of essentially decent men who can fearlessly die fighting even for a few inches of land claimed by their government. The officers are shown to be Anglicized, but in love with more or less traditional Indian women. All of them are chivalrous and good natured. Vijay Anand is shown on leave at the beginning of the film singing melody, in Rafi's romantic voice, while driving an army jeep all by himself on the winding and picturesque Leh-Srinagar road. Although the song refers to Anand's beloved fiancé pining away for him in Srinagar, its larger visual significance does not elude us. The landscape on which the jeep, a metaphor of dominating masculinity, is being driven is barren and forms a safe playground for the cocky and careless bourgeois officer. The geographical and cultural penetration of the remote Ladakhi desert by the Westernized Indian elite is illuminated further with the help of Western dance sequences within the song which firmly establish the Western (read modern) cultural orientation of the army officers. The coy fiancé, however, is shown appropriately dressed in a salwar-kameez and *sari*, thus signifying the gender difference in the appropriation of a problematic modernity. The dance sequences within the song are metaphors of dominant middle-class cultural practices.

While crossing Sonamarg, he witnesses young Captain Bahadur Singh (Dharmendra) busy converting a local juvenile into an infantryman. Soon after, Bahadur, true to his name, responds to the helpless heroine's distress call and rescues a lamb from the edge of a cliff, thus affirming the humane character of Indian Army officers. Love blossoms almost immediately between the two. Incidentally, the heroine (Priya Rajvansh) is the elder sister of the lad undergoing tough military training in Bahadur's hands. This love finds parental, and more importantly maternal, stamp of approval from Bahadur's side rather quickly in the film; his mother agrees to accept a mountain flower growing wild in the Ladakh desert as her daughter-in-law. The chivalry of officers is attested to by another sequence in which Balraj Sahni, the Major, escorts the heroine, her mother and the adolescent soldier in his jeep all the way to Leh from Sonamarg. Towards the end of the film when false news of Bahadur's death is conveyed to Sahni's beleaguered camp of survivors, he actually proposes marriage to the heroine–an offer she politely turns down like a model Indian woman.

The *jawans* are more realistically depicted as hopeless young patriots destined to die. But in defeat and death something more is said for them. They are rescued from the danger of being perceived as mere cannon fodder in a war not of their making. One way in which this is done is by showing the friendship between men and their officers, and the integration of the former with the nationalist rhetoric of the latter. Documentary footage of Nehru addressing masses of *jawans* is deliberately used in the film to enhance its emotive nationalist appeal.[15] The drawing upon of Nehru's mass popularity is contraposed to the cunning of the Chinese to which there are repeated, and expected, references in the film. In fact, the film begins by blanking out the contemporary background of the border dispute. At the start an incorrect voiceover asserts that the story of the film begins in July 1962 'when the Chinese aggression seemed unthinkable' and ends in November 1962 'when the first attack was over and the second was just a few days away'.[16] Unlike some critical views of Nehru's China policy the film's message is clear: here is/was our dear well-meaning leader who was led astray and betrayed by the covetous Chinese. At another level gender is deliberately evoked to place the predicament of life and death of *jawans* in perspective. The nation's sympathies for them are sought to be stimulated by their separation from their families, wives and girlfriends to which songs, conversations, showing of photographs and the receiving of letters from home constantly alludes. A soldier defending the motherland on the battlefield, it is implied, thinks of home, women and love and, therefore, society, in turn, should think of him.

The heroic love plot in *Haqeeqat* presents an interesting phenomenon. It actually narrates a tale of Ladakh's unambiguous union with the Indian Republic. Otherwise what was the need to throw a local girl and her family into the picture? A Kashmiri-Ladakhi local (Priya Rajvansh) is shown to be in love with an Indian Army officer, Captain Bahadur Singh (played by Dharmendra and patterned on Major Shaitan Singh of the 13th Battalion, Kumaon Regiment), who is the son of a senior Indian officer played by Jayant. The evolution of the girl's character, journey and denouement in the film appends a subtext of national integration to the overall nationalism of the venture. The material superiority of the Indian mainstream in this process of integration is highlighted by Bahadur's offer of giving the girl plenty of clothes and jewellery after marriage in the city. He asks her enthusiastically whether she would like all this and she says yes with equal pleasure in a moment signifying upward social mobility. The willingness of the locals to integrate with India represented by officers drawn from its ruling classes, is thus established. The short-lived love which grows between this girl born of mixed Kashmiri-Ladakhi parentage and a manly Hindu Indian officer from the plains is symbolic of India's national integration. Interestingly, and following the bourgeois colonizing tendency of Bollywood referred to earlier, no *jawan* is shown in love with a local girl. It is as if only the officers have a right to mix with locals and, if possible, appropriate their beautiful girls with the help of the military infrastructure and leisure at their disposal. Matters are made easier for Bahadur, as well as the Major who flirts with the heroine while driving her to Leh, by the absence of the girl's father, a potential patriarchal opponent, from the scene. This deliberate absence is not without sexual, communal and nationalist implications[10]. Towards the end of the film both the girl and her lover die fighting the Chinese in a last desperate stand. The attitude which the nomads are shown displaying towards the Indian Army is calculated to valorize the latter. It is designed to tell us that the locals have accepted the Indians, represented by their well-behaved *jawans* and handsome officers, and their notions of India's territorial spread and integrity. The film also refers to, and indeed shows, the raising of a Ladakhi militia and even local women, including the heroine, receiving rifle-training to reinforce the point.

The Ladakhis' loyalty to India is also buttressed by scenes towards the end of the film in which the heroine, on her way to meet and deliver a message to Bahadur Singh, is captured by a Chinese patrol. Then, in some of the crudest images employed by the film, her clothes are ripped off and she is raped by a Chinese junior officer played by a Bollywood junior artiste of Nepali origin. Before this rape, which in typical Hindi film fashion involves the breaking of her bangles under the ammunition boots of the Chinese soldiers holding her down (this could be interpreted to mean: (a) the loss of her virginity, and (b) a premonition of her lover's impending death), she is interrogated by a senior Chinese officer about sensitive Indian positions.[18] The officer also offers her a thousand rupees–a princely sum for a Ladakhi in 1962–for her cooperation after shouting the routine *Hindi-Chini bhai bhai* slogan. She stoically refuses and ultimately dies fighting beside her lover some minutes later in the film. These are overtly propagandist parts of the film in which the Chinese are shown to be greedy, cruel and disrespectful to women and locals in general. To prove that the Chinese are avaricious and brutal they are shown trampling over dead *jawans* and robbing them of their valuables like wrist watches. In a symbolic act of insulting the Indian motherland one of them kicks a sweetmeat tin containing soil and flowers grown from seeds sent by a *jawan*'s wife. However, this insult is avenged almost immediately when a dying Indian soldier shoots the offender. Before all this happens the husband is shown successfully growing some flowers in the tin and offering them to his officer (Vijay Anand).

The involvement of the locals makes a specific point in the film. The makers of the film had the option of keeping either the locals out of it or showing them as neutrals in a war being fought for their territory by outsiders on both sides. The latter the Censor Board would never have cleared. There are reasons why they chose to depict the nomads as being loyal to India's cause in the film. It can be surmised easily that the producer-director had the example of Kashmiri responses to the Indian Army during the Pakistani incursion of 1948 to fall back on. Hence, there was no harm in inserting similar local responses to serve the cause of Indian nationalism and territorial claims on the Sino-Indian border. Showing the locals supporting the Indian Army was most probably done to justify further India's claim to some disputed territory on the Sino-Indian border. At the beginning of the film, when the Major drives the heroine and her family to Leh (to which Bahadur Singh is also quickly and conveniently posted) the family, by way of a clearly contrived question-answer conversation with the Major, informs him of the geographical and social spread of their community from Sonamarg to places beyond Chushul. This has obvious implications for demarcating the Kashmiri-Ladakhi side of the border dispute and simultaneously underplaying the possible existence of friction between the Kashmiris and Ladakhis.

The assumptions underlying the help rendered to the Indian Army by the Ladakhi gypsies make for an interesting story. In this connection what is left unsaid in the film shores up Indian claims on the disputed border. In the film the nomads have already taken sides in a conflict they purportedly understand; their sympathies are shown to naturally lie with the Indians, although racially perhaps they are closer to the 'invaders' in terms of race defined by the imagery and dialogues contained in the film itself. Is there a veiled suggestion in the film that the border tribes are aware of the historical nature of the border dispute? Is it implied that the Tibetans' dislike of Chinese expansion into Tibet spills over into Ladakh? The ease with which the locals fit into the Indian scheme of things points to their having taken 'our' side even before the conflict degenerates into war. The Tibetan reaction and resistance to the Chinese conquest, and India's support to the Dalai Lama, must certainly have underpinned such assumptions. The arrival of Tibetan refugees in Ladakh and other parts of north India during the 1950s was obviously a part of the context informing the making of *Haqeeqat*. The rejection and othering of the Communist Chinese translates easily into the acceptance of Indian claims leaving the border tribes with little choice. The self-righteous bottom-line, buttressed by bombastic civilizational phraseology uttered by important characters in the film, is that, since 'we' are better than the God-less Communist Chinese, the trans-border tribes better run along with us. The fact that the Indian Army could have been viewed, and, therefore, also probably disliked, by at least some locals as the inheritor of British colonialism in the area escaped the filmmakers' nationalist attentions completely. The gypsies' close identification with the Indian state is a ploy used to justify the territorial claims of the Government of India which, in different conditions, has been a known oppressor of marginal tribes in the interest of the social mainstream. It helps to portray the Indian Army in true heroic colours–an army supported by the locals and by default also *their* army defying the unjust invader unto death. The tragic death of the local beauty alongside Indian soldiers symbolizes the ultimate acceptance of the Indian Union by the border tribes, even as her love affair with Bahadur Singh, a martial north Indian as his surname suggests, symbolizes the vertical social assimilation of the marginal with the mainstream. Hence, *Haqeeqat* ends up becoming a tribute to the colonization of the remotest corners of South Asia by the Indian middle-class in the name of civilization, modernity and nationalism.

NOTES

1. Parts of this chapter are drawn from Anirudh Deshpande, *Class Power and Consciousness in Indian Cinema and Television*. New Delhi: Primus Books, 2009 (Paperback editions in 2013 and 2015).
2. From the Introduction of Arthur Marwick (ed.), *Total War and Social Change*. London: Macmillan, 1988.

3. Camera Obscura, *Hindustan Times*, New Delhi, October 2, 2003.
4. This is in striking contrast to the practice of getting service widows remarried, sometimes in publicized ceremonies, encouraged by the state. Whether this is done to actually help the widows in question or in the interest of augmenting the supply of recruits in the long run remains a matter of speculation.
5. The message of Upkaar is not entirely anti-urban. The urban is redeemed through the medium of gender in the character of the lady doctor (Asha Parekh) who ultimately marries Bharat (Manoj Kumar) and presumably settles down in the village. Thus India meets Bharat and loses itself in the culturally superior latter.
6. Miriam Bratu Hansen, 'Schindler's List is Not Shoah: The Second Commandment, Popular Modernism and Public Memory', in Marcia Landy, *The Historical Film: History and Memory in Media*, The Athlone Press, London, 2001. Critics of the film have argued that it shows the Jews from the German perspective and is 'concerned with survival, the survival of individuals, rather than the fact of death, the death of an entire people of peoples' (p. 205). Hansen cites other critics of the film to this effect. From her reading of the film it becomes clear that while Spielberg concentrates on evolving Schindler's role from the banal to heroic, the Jewish characters in the film appear more or less stereotyped. This, most unfortunately, falls in line with Jew caricaturing central to anti-Semitism.
7. *Haqeeqat* was produced by Himalaya Films and directed by Chetan Anand. Its hit music was scored by Madan Mohan and the stirring lyrics were by Kaifi Azmi. The impressive star cast comprised Balraj Sahni, Jayant, Dharmendra, Vijay Anand, Priya Rajvansh, Indrani Mukherjee, Sanjay Khan, Chand Usmani, Achala Sachdev, Gulab, Sulochana and Sudhir. Among the junior artistes in the film were Gurung, the stereotyped Nepali chowkidar of Hindi cinema who plays a Chinese officer, and MacMohan who later gained fame as Gabbar Singh's henchman Samba in Sholay. The songs of the film sung by Mohammad Rafi, Talat Mehmood, Manna De, Bhupendra and Lata Mangeshkar remain popular till today.

8. Yves Thoraval, *The Cinemas of India*. Macmillan, 2000, p. 113.
9. The British had fashioned the theory of the Indian martial races in their belief in ruling India with the help of a yeoman peasantry. This alliance of a paternal colonial state and its martial supporters was supposedly forged against political India with its urban and middle-class character. After independence the Indian middle class substituted the British in this arrangement which was made to work against external threats, namely Pakistan and China. Nationalist ideology plays an important role in keeping this arrangement intact in a domestic context informed by growing class and caste discontent and conflict. The Hindu nationalists desire to make this military arrangement work against the 'other' (read religious minorities, especially Muslims) defined both within and outside India. The danger this poses to the professionalism of the Indian Army and maintenance of internal peace is easy to perceive. Turning the *jawan* against the 'other' in India will not consolidate but destroy India. In this context we must also note the steep decline in the number of Muslims serving in the Indian armed forces since 1947.
10. The local girl's father, for instance, could become the symbol of community resistance to an Indian officer interested in her, thus jeopardizing the petty bourgeois nationalist project. His control over the girl's sexuality could pose problems for the more powerful males represented by the Captain and Major. This would have created avoidable diversions in a nationalist plot in which the sexual expropriation of a local girl is the metaphor for the integration of localities into the more mainstream nation. In many Hindi films overcoming the local girl's father plays an important part in the plot centred on the hero's or even the comedian's socio-sexual conquest. In most of the films the girl's father is a weak male compared with either the villain or hero seeking her sexual favours. Quite often the villain is shown exercising some power over the father. In *Haqeeqat* the role of this weak father-male is taken over by the girl's younger brother who is completely impressed by the officers and goes about saluting them smartly whenever an occasion arises.

6

History and Revolutionary-Deconstruction: Ambedkar's Historical Method

> There is nothing that I have urged in support of my thesis which I have asked my readers to accept on trust. I have at least shown that there exists a preponderance of probability in favour of what I have asserted. *It would be nothing but pedantry to say that a preponderance of probability is not a sufficient basis for a valid decision*... I am not so vain as to claim any finality for my thesis... my critics [should] consider whether this thesis is not a workable and therefore, for the time being, a valid hypothesis *if the test of a valid hypothesis is that it should fit in with all surrounding facts, explain them and give them a meaning which in its absence they do not appear to have.* I do not want anything more from my critics than a fair and unbiased appraisal. [Emphasis Added]
>
> –B.R. Ambedkar, Preface to *The Untouchables*, 1948.

This chapter presents a commentary on Ambedkar's historical method. It is based on the presumption that as a legacy of his prodigious intellect his historical approach to politics has, so far, not been acknowledged as it should be by the establishment of Indian historians. I don't remember my respected Marxist professors referring to him as a historian during my student days at the Centre for Historical Studies, JNU, during the 1980s–one of the premier centres for historical researches in India. The Marxists of CHS were usually sympathetic to the Indian National Congress and therefore not happy with Dalit or Left perspectives critical of India's freedom movement. Consequently, their students were made more familiar with Nehru's soft Left writings than the works of radical scholars like Ambedkar or Periyar. Dalit scholars and activists often do not get along very well with the Marxists and this was the case with Ambedkar too. It is well known that Ambedkar was both an admirer and critic of Marxism and this aspect of his historical method has been highlighted by my friend Professor Umesh Bagade in a well written tract[1]. His differences with the Marxists stemmed from various points. One, he was critical of historical materialism because of its tendency to accord primacy to economics in its worldview. Two, in Ambedkar's view, caste struggle in India was more important than class struggle. This was so because of the historical difference between Indian and European society. And finally, Ambedkar reasoned that to change the superstructure is as important as to change the base of society. In sum, he reasoned that only the annihilation of caste would pave the way for a socialist transformation of Indian society. I call Ambedkar a socialist because he championed social justice and equity but the route to socialism he chose for himself and his followers ran through the fields of caste discrimination. The Marxists of his day were mostly Brahmins who followed the Soviet definition of Marxism coloured by the views of Stalin. Today this definition is usually called orthodox Marxism. In the 1920s, 30s and 40s Indian Marxists remained focused on class to the detriment of caste struggles and this alienated them from Ambedkar who was an organic intellectual of the depressed castes. The inability of the Indian Marxists of his time to jettison their dogmatic approach to Indian history and politics put him off. His understanding of Indian and European history convinced him that the masses were not as passive as the 'positivist' Marxists held them to be. In contrast to the orthodox Marxists he placed his hope in human agency and the ability of ideas to change history. Whether the history of India since 1947 proves him right or wrong is a different matter.

I do not remember Ambedkar being considered seriously as a historian in college or university. Even in the Department of History, Delhi University, where I have taught history to post-graduate and research students since 2009, Ambedkar is usually not recognized as a historian despite the deep historicity of his overall work on the Indian caste system. This state of affairs has come to pass because of the following causes. First, the questions of caste and untouchability, in general, have not been accorded the importance they deserve in Indian historiography despite the rise of the Subaltern Studies in the 1980s and 1990s. In the Indian social sciences matters of caste are generally dealt with by sociologists or anthropologists. Historians therefore depend on *their* works to fortify historical generalizations. Two, most Indian history departments teach historical methodology in a Eurocentric context. The 'models' of history writing included in their methodology and theory curriculum are usually Western; Whig, Utilitarian, Marxist, Prussian, Annales, Structuralist, Post-Structuralist, Post-Modern, etc. This in itself is not unproductive but leaves little scope to teach historical methods arising from modern Indian thinkers like Phule, Periyar and Ambedkar. For instance, whenever Indian history departments raise the importance of hermeneutics they may refer to R.G. Collingwood or William Dilthey or Martin Heidegger but never a tradition of modern Indian hermeneutics going back to at least Jyotiba Phule in the 19th century. This chapter seeks a redress of this imbalance by drawing attention to the immense hermeneutic potential of Ambedkar's writings on caste and other political and economic matters. It proceeds on the assumption that in engaging with the theory and structure of caste and the problem of untouchability in India, Ambedkar had pioneered a constructive method of deconstruction long before the relativism and subjectivism of post-modernism and deconstruction developed by anti-Marxist philosophers like Michel Foucault and Jacques Derrida confounded the practice of history writing post-1945. We have alluded to some of this confusion in Chapter one. By the 1980s an influential section of Indian social scientists, including historians, were affected by the linguistic, cultural and feminist turns. In such conditions the question of taking Ambedkar seriously as a historian did not arise. In the 1950s, 60s and 70s he was not paid enough attention because the nationalists and Marxists held sway over Indian historiography. The Dalit and tribal question made these scholars uncomfortable. To the nationalist the nation, and to the Marxists class remained central; both tended to underestimate the proper role of caste difference and discrimination in Indian history and the specific problems of the *Antyaja Jatis*.

To understand Ambedkar as a historian a visit to the intellectual climate of late colonial India is necessary. This period of Indian history was dominated by the rise of nationalism(s) which either militated against colonialism or each other. Since these ideologies were socially aggregative in character and objective they usually undermined the divisiveness and oppression caused in Indian society by caste. The writing of history followed this political trend. Further, it was unusual for Indian historians to debate questions of historical methods in the 1940s; the official archive and colonial historical methods reigned supreme over their imagination and the difference between the Imperialist and Nationalist historians was one of objectives and not methods. Most Indian historians were content with the canons of historiography taught to them by their British professors who, in turn, were mostly Whig in orientation. The Indian nationalist historians of all hues wrote history with the help of these canons which had influenced their minds in favour of Western historiography. Perhaps some exceptions to this rule were the Marxists, like D.D. Kosambi, who applied Marxism and fieldwork to the study of Indian history in the first few decades of the 20th century. Notwithstanding the remarkable advance in historical insights achieved by the Indian Marxists much of their work concentrated on the working class as a class to the detriment of caste-based studies. The existence of class, based on economic relations in Indian society, was usually accepted uncritically by the Indian Marxists. Indian historiography in the 1940s rarely dealt with the questions of caste, tribe and gender which were generally left to the sociologists. The model of Sanskritization emanated from Indian sociology and underestimated the contradictory nature of caste relations in the Indian everyday life. B.R. Ambedkar's innovative views on the conception of, and writing, history appear nothing less than astonishing in this context. At a time when the 'salt and pepper' professional Indian historians like Sir Jadunath Sarkar rarely ventured beyond the narratives of historical individuals and events in their writings, Ambedkar reflected on those aspects of historiography which exercise our minds today. He conceived history as a synthesis of art, science and story-telling underscored by the historian's fertile and creative imagination as early as 1948 when history departments in the Indian universities rarely taught historiography as a subject unto itself; history innocently existed in the official archive for them to be discovered and narrated as professionally as possible. In this context his suggestion that the historian must be self-conscious in the task of raising scientific consciousness among his readers rings true for all time. The fact that only by a conscious critical engagement with his sources, which in Ambedkar's case comprised the texts produced by Brahmans and Buddhists in Ancient India, could social history as a subject be conceived underlines his entire corpus of writing. Since the historian always makes an argument his view of the sources can never be informed by a simple positivism which drives history towards individuals and events to the detriment of the interpretative contexts within which they are always located. Today when we speak of a possible hermeneutics of caste we must remember and read Ambedkar's texts on the subject.

Dr. B.R. Ambedkar's legacy thrives in an intriguing intellectual and political milieu. His differences with the Congress, on questions of caste and the Congress leaders' attitudes towards the *Dalits* and other matters like the Hindu Code Bill, have not deterred the Congress leaders from manufacturing and appropriating a false image of him. Since its rout in the 2014 Parliament Elections the Congress is hard pressed to regain its image as India's premier centrist-liberal party. Therefore, it is desperate to claim Ambedkar primarily as a constitutional expert. It is true that Ambedkar collaborated with Nehru in laying down the foundations of post-colonial India but this collaboration between two modernists should not make us gloss over the fundamental differences between Ambedkar's politics and the Gandhian morality which guided the Congress at least till 1947. On the other hand, the Hindutva forces which rule India today are trying to appropriate Ambedkar to their cause. In 1997 the right wing journalist Arun Shourie had called Ambedkar a pro-British false god unworthy of worship. Now that position is passé. These days the BJP-RSS wants to convert the millions of Bahujan followers of Babasaheb to its mission of creating a Hindu Rashtra. At the same time the Indian state and the educational institutions, under Hindutva influence, continue the policy of persecuting and ostracizing Dalit students and activists. The new found BJP love for Ambedkar demonstrates nothing but the politics of symbolism. The Hindutva ideologues know that a Hindu Rashtra in India cannot be created by *only* alienating and demonizing the Muslims. The BJP's 2015 defeat in Bihar, preceded as it was by the tactless pronouncements of the arrogant RSS chief on reservations, forced it to reconsider its hostility to Ambedkar. However, the impressive electoral success of the BJP in Uttar Pradesh in 2017 and the appointment of a religious leader as the state's Chief Minister has infused more energy in the anti-Dalit Hindutva forces in the state. Despite these developments the symbolic RSS appropriation of Ambedkar proceeds in line with the objectives of the Hindu Rashtra. However, these selective misleading appropriations of Ambedkar do not square with his critical reading of Indian history; Babasaheb neither squares with the RSS nor Congress. His criticism of the Congress and the Hindu Mahasabha are too well known to be repeated here. Ambedkar collaborated with Nehru in the creation of the Indian constitution as a member of the Constituent Assembly but when the time to hand over the constitution to the people of India came he spoke prophetic words. He told the Indians that their society was feudal and democracy in a feudal caste-ridden society can only be a window dressing. In saying that a constitution is only as good as the people who become its guardians he almost predicted the moral decline which would swamp India not long after independence.

The attempted political misappropriations of Ambedkar necessitate periodic visits to his multifarious and prodigious intellect. So far he has been examined and accepted as an expert on the Indian caste system, the politics of constitutionalism and an organic intellectual of the Indian untouchable and lower castes. There is no doubt that these are germane aspects of his overall thought but I would argue that the sum total of his razor sharp intellect exceeds these achievements and rises to a level of philosophical reasoning rarely achieved by learned Indians in colonial and even post-colonial India. His belief in the universal Enlightenment values made him a modernist and a lifelong adversary of *Sanatan* Hinduism–there was no room for a flirtation with romanticism, superstition or mystical in his historical vision. In this he differed from the nationalists who believed in a 'golden age' of Indian history in the hoary past. He was of the belief that God did not create society and its various grotesque features like caste and untouchability. His critical understanding of Indian history also negated the sentimentality which Gandhi demonstrated for the Hindu *Varnashramdharma* and the idyllic pre-modern village–clearly a myth suited to *Savarna* hegemony and the notion of *Ramrajya*. All this makes the appropriation of Ambedkar by the Congress from a liberal-Hindu viewpoint impossible; Ambedkar viewed the Indian society and village from the viewpoint of the oppressed castes. Unlike Gandhi and other Congress leaders he did not favor caste reconciliation but desired the complete abolition of caste. Gandhi, for instance, favoured a reform of the caste system but not its abolition. In contrast Ambedkar's objective was the abolition of the caste system. Gandhi was a reformer from above, Ambedkar a revolutionary from below.

The historical *explanation* of India offered by both men differed in accordance with their political objectives.

This brief intervention in the omnipresent vexed dialogue which post-colonial Indian modernity has with Ambedkar asserts that his profound engagement with the universal and scientific values of the Enlightenment, with a mix of dialectics, logic and reason at their centre, made him an "anti-myth" historian par excellence much before history moved in the direction of becoming a critical discipline in select Indian universities post 1947[2]. His writings as a historian and essayist, pace Voltaire, Goethe and Gorky who influenced his thinking, are too critical of the Hindu religion and therefore cannot be appropriated by the descendants of those whom he criticized with an academic rigour rare in his day. In his hands the craft of history assumed a unique ambition; the destruction of an unjust order based on caste distinctions. Since his politics were a product of his unsentimental vision of Indian history and vice versa, his historical views and method need a reappraisal in the context of a cow-worshipping, caste valorizing and anti-Dalit Vedic paligenetic nationalism which governs popular historical imagination in the times of globalization[3]. The *Annihilation of Caste* and several of his rigorously argued essays places him in the rich tradition of counter-culture omnipresent, but under-taught, in India.

A full examination of Ambedkar's writings, spread over thousands of pages, from the viewpoint of discovering him as a historian is beyond the scope of this chapter. Though such an enterprise might prove fruitful in future, at hand I have one text, *The Untouchables*, the preface of which comprises a succinct comment on the historical method followed by Ambedkar as he set out to deconstruct the scriptural shibboleths of caste and thereby the basis of Hinduism[4]. This essay can be read as a commentary on that brilliant Preface this author stumbled across while cobbling together a new reading list for his MPhil class on research methodology. The essays in *The Untouchables* and the method of history outlined in its Preface demonstrate at least three crucial attributes of Ambedkar's historical thought.

One, and here we are reminded of the idea of history visualized by R.G. Collingwood, Babasaheb's historical inquiries began with contemporary political questions directly related to power. This political approach to history places him in the category of scholars like Karl Marx, Antonio Gramsci and Paul Thompson for whom the study of history, i.e. the examination of causes, consequences and discourse, was related to the exercise of power and its legitimization by the ruling classes. Why should we read history? To better understand the present and thereby create a better tomorrow for humanity. That would have been Ambedkar's answer. In this scheme of things history does not become a profession. It becomes the necessary tool for our emancipation from the myths which cloud our minds and prevent clear headed thinking. History emerges from our political struggle as a critical vocation. The tension and resolution of social contradiction is central to this historical approach. The primary political questions, and the dominant view of a subject pertinent to them, exercised Ambedkar's intellect and he embarked on a vigorous mental journey to answer them. Second, and in this respect Ambedkar's method came close to his contemporary, and the founder of the Annales School, Marc Bloch, was his pursuit of a regressive method of historical analysis. His historiography was interdisciplinary. Its objective was to prove or disprove generalizations regarding the present and possible future of Indian society. His salutary research aim was to show how the present was produced by the past–there is no room for studying the past for its own sake or entertainment in his historiography. The mythology of the nation or community is absent from his work. His view of Indian society was structural and caste appears in it as a *longue duree* factor [long-term historical phenomena].[5] Caste is both the base and superstructure of Indian society; both relations of production and power are mediated through it. His essays confirm his deep understanding of the interaction of the past and the present–the hallmark of a good historian forever alert to the politics of his age. Three, his essays convey his fertile historical imagination and superb command over language-qualities essential to the practice of any meaningful social science. Here it should be remembered that while specializing in Economics at Columbia he had read history and sociology as ancillary subjects. This inter-disciplinary training enriched his approach to the problems of inequality in

Indian society throughout his career. His insightful essays prove that he applied a lawyer's skill of cross examination to the sources of history and tradition to arrive at conclusions with which it is difficult to disagree. Some of these conclusions may appear dated or over-stated today but that in no way diminishes the hermeneutic method he used to arrive at them. His rigorous sociological analysis of Indian mythology, for example, is a lesson to Indian historians.

In Bagade's words:

> Ambedkar took recourse to mythology to write the history of caste-varna struggles of India. His approach towards myth was twofold. Firstly, he indulged in the materialist interpretations of the myths and provided a discerning portrayal of Indian social history. Secondly, like Phule, he provided a devastating critique of myths and their mythical heroes. He employed more advanced methods than Phule to produce facts from the myths. He juxtaposed different versions of the same myth from different texts and deduced facts from them. He gathered corroborative evidence from other sources or authorities in support of these facts. And then he situated these corroborated facts in their context of social process or in the course of probability to establish their veracity. Ambedkar's method of analyzing myth is exemplified in his work *Who Were the Shudras?*[6]

Since Ambedkar's becoming a historian of Indian society was intimately connected with his negation of caste and thereby the Hindu religion he began the Preface by coming to the point straightaway by raising the political question which inspired his historical research. The Preface shows that what Marx is to Capitalism, Ambedkar is to Hinduism; to the former the relations of production produced by the Capitalism comprised the core of any meaningful analysis of capitalism and to the latter caste was at the heart of the relations of power which sustained *Sanatan* Hinduism. According to the Preface the "Hindu Civilization" is "a diabolical contrivance to suppress and enslave humanity. Its proper name would be Infamy." Furthermore, the Hindus, throughout history, had neither searched for nor rationally investigated the origin of their own civilization, i.e. the *varna-jati* system. Hence the first question: Why did the Hindu not scientifically investigate his so-called civilization? This non examination, in his view, happened because the Hindu did not consider the existence of the caste system and untouchability a "matter of apology or shame." He felt "no responsibility either to atone for it or to enquire into its origin and growth." Further, and reminiscent of what Alberuni wrote of the Hindus in his *India*, he explains that "every Hindu is taught to believe that his civilization is not only the most ancient but that it is also in many respects altogether unique. No Hindu ever feels tired of repeating these claims...The inculcation of these false beliefs in the sanity, superiority and sanctity of Hindu Civilization is due entirely to the peculiar social psychology of Hindu scholars." [emphasis added]. This social psychology was a product of the long-term pedagogical hegemony wielded by the Brahmans in India since time immemorial. This hegemony had given them a scriptural and ritual authority in Indian society and, it may be added, this scriptural-ritual authority was reinforced, *inter alia*, by British rule in India. The Brahmans were learned men no doubt, but not intellectuals in the true sense of the term. To understand the unenlightened approach of these learned men to their own historical condition Ambedkar delved into comparative history and the history of ideas. "Today" he mentioned in 1948 "all scholarship is confined to the Brahmins. But unfortunately no Brahmin scholar has so far come forward to play the part of a Voltaire who had the intellectual honesty to rise against the doctrines of the Catholic Church in which he was brought up; nor is one likely to appear on the scene in future. It is a grave reflection on the scholarship of the Brahmins that they should not have produced a Voltaire." For an intellectual to arise and gain respect in society certain necessary and sufficient historical conditions must obtain; these conditions were absent from Indian history. Critical introspection of the self happens in peculiar historical circumstances and the Brahmins, by virtue of their addiction to their traditional learning, had proved themselves incapable of such an effort. Therefore, the Brahmin scholar was "only a learned man" and "not an intellectual" though he claimed to be a social reformer in colonial conditions; on closer inspection this claim appeared false. The differences between upper caste led social reform movements in 19th century India and the subversive path chosen by Jyotiba and Savitribai Phule comes to mind here. Having written this, Ambedkar drew upon European history and the *Enlightenment* to dilate on the meaning of the word *intellectual*: "There is a world of difference between one who is learned and one who is an intellectual. The former is class-conscious and is alive to the interests of his class. The latter is an emancipated being who is free to act without being swayed by class considerations. It is because the Brahmins have been only learned men that they have not produced a Voltaire" [Emphasis Added]. The ability of an individual to grasp objective reality with the help of critical thought was central to this *Enlightenment* informed approach to society and history. The difference between subject and object was central to the philosophy of Ambedkar; he did not oppose caste just because he was a Mahar but because he was genuinely enlightened.

According to Ambedkar the only way to disprove the unreasonable assertions of the Brahmins and the so-called scholars aligned with them was to raise questions and answer them by developing a "new way of looking at old things." Admittedly his own answers to the questions raised by untouchability in India were a "result" of the "historical research" he conducted. Further, he consciously followed the ideal of objective history writing laid down by the German statesman-historian-philosopher-poet Johann Wolfgang von Goethe with whose maxims and reflections he was familiar. According to Goethe's prescription the historian's duty is to "separate the true from the false, the certain from the uncertain, and the doubtful from that which cannot be accepted." For a historian, serving on the jury was a juridical metaphor for Goethe which Ambedkar took seriously: "Every investigator must before all things look upon himself as one who is summoned to serve on a jury. He has only to consider how far the statement of the case is complete and clearly set forth by the evidence. Then he draws his conclusion and gives his vote, whether it be that his opinion coincides with that of the foreman or not."

Goethe inspired but did not constrain Ambedkar. The latter was alert to the possibility of missing links arising in the study of the past events. In a country like India this was quite likely. What should the historian do in cases where "relevant and necessary facts" and "direct evidence of connected relations between important events" are not available to him? Should he stop working "until the link is discovered?" Ambedkar's answer to this question is a valid negation of academic pedantism:

> I believe that in such cases it is permissible for him to use his imagination and intuition to bridge the gaps left in the chain of facts by links not yet discovered and to propound a working hypothesis suggesting how facts which cannot be connected by known facts might have been interconnected.

The point, according to Ambedkar, was not to quibble over the distinction between direct and inferential evidence to examine whether a thesis violated "the canons of historical research" but to avoid a "thesis based on pure conjecture." Thus the difference between creative imagination and fantasy was maintained in his historical method. The crucial difference between pure conjecture and a possible thesis led him to a deconstruction of the sources to "divine what the texts conceal" and the "task of gathering survivals of the past, placing them together and making them tell the story of their birth."

This work of the historian, in Ambedkar's words, is:

> analogous to that of the archaeologist who constructs a city from broken stones or of the paleontologist who conceives an extinct animal from scattered bones and teeth or of a painter who reads the line of the horizon and the smallest vestiges on the slopes of the hill to make up a scene. In this sense the book is a work of art even more than history...It cannot but be that imagination and hypothesis should play a large part in such a work. But that in itself cannot be a ground for the

> condemnation of the thesis. For without trained imagination no scientific inquiry can be fruitful and hypothesis is the very soul of science.

Concluding Remarks

In conclusion it can be said that the revolutionary philosophy of Ambedkar was predicated upon a patient, laborious and critical reading of the primary sources he selected to fashion a rational argument debunking the caste system in general and untouchability in particular. His articles prove that deconstructing the discourse of the ruling classes/castes is the primary objective of the historian. By claiming no "finality" for his thesis and underlining the difference between pure conjecture and theoretical possibilities in a system of historical analysis, Ambedkar pioneered an *open ended* approach to social history at a time when most Indian historians rarely ventured beyond the ideology of nationalism and the battlefields of the past. Ambedkar's historical method remains resilient and alluring in our times because his reflections highlighted the important political difference between imagination and fantasy, conjecture and possibility and a credible story and academic pedantry in the formulation of his historical submissions. As a modernist he desired rational knowledge and a new egalitarian society, and not another myth, to replace the sophistry of the establishment. Hence the task of deconstructing the ideology of Indian society did not begin and end with deconstruction in his thought. Reading a text critically was a means to a political end for Ambedkar and not an end in itself as it has become in much of anti-Marxist theory since 1945; deconstructing the ideological representation of history was crucial to his mission of reconstructing a new progressive society. The question of power remained important to him, and, like Lenin and other revolutionary intellectuals, he did not evince a cynical view of power which became the hallmark of the post-modern approach to power after 1945. He urged his followers to read, criticize what they read and evolve a new way of life based on a rational critique of the past. He worked in an age when the Prussian straight jacket of Leopold von Ranke was worn with aplomb by the professional historians of India and the method of positivism reigned supreme over their narrow pretentiously apolitical minds. To accept and validate history as a credible artistic and scientific story told by the imaginative historian on the basis of a critical reading of contemporary and historical sources in 1948 was to anticipate many future and exciting developments in historiography. It is a pity that Ambedkar has been, perhaps unwittingly or conveniently, reduced to a "Dalit" intellectual-philosopher in the Indian schools and universities. Indeed, this anti-myth Indian pioneer of revolutionary deconstruction should have been taken seriously by this country's fraternity of Historians decades ago. That would have given history writing a different purpose in a country obsessed with national and regional identities and the projection of these on the past.

NOTES

1. *Ambedkar's Historical Method.* New Delhi: Critical Quest, 2015.
2. Dorothy M. Fugeira's characterization of Phule and Ambedkar in *Aryans, Jews Brahmins: Theorizing Authority Through Myths of Identity*. New Delhi: Navayana, 2015.
3. The word paligenetic means the discovery of an ancient mythical romanticized nation in the hoary past. In some senses all nationalisms are paligenetic but Fascist and Nazi nations, following Roger Griffin's submissions on the subject, more so.
4. Dr. B.R. Ambedkar, *The Untouchables.* Delhi: Siddharth Books, 2008 [First Published 1948].
5. The concept of *longue duree* was pioneered by the French Annales historians. It refers to the long-term influences on human history like geography but some scholars include culture in this definition. According to the French historian Fernand Braudel, geography, demography and economy comprised the *longue duree* but scholars also insist that mentality, i.e. cultural attitudes which would include caste in India, is also a long-term phenomenon which changes imperceptibly.
6. *Ambedkar's Historical Method*, p. 19.

7

The Individual and History: A Note on Shivaji Maharaj (February 19, 1630-April 3, 1680)

> Islam and Hinduism are only different pigments used by the Divine Painter to picture the human species. To show bigotry for any man's creed and practices is to alter the words of the Holy Book.
>
> –Shivaji to Aurangzeb, 1679[1]

> It is not true that Shivaji succeeded because he believed in the Hindu religion. Evidence suggests that he set out to do something better for the world than merely save his religion.
>
> –Govind Pansare[2]

Historians often have to answer an important question. What is the role of an individual in history? This question is usually asked with reference to known kings and queens, politicians, statesmen, generals, conquerors, scientists and so on who are supposed to have guided and changed the course of human history in some way or the other. The question is irrelevant to lay individuals who, it is assumed, are born, live and die without making a difference to history. In my view this assumption is not ill founded because people as individuals really make an insignificant impact on history. The answer to the question is easy. There are exceptional individuals who, given congenial historical circumstances, wield power and usher in social and economic changes in a country's or region's history. On closer inspection it might be found that many such men or women were products of historical forces already present in strength in the societies which produced them at an opportune moment. Thus we locate men like Alexander, Caesar, Changez Khan, Akbar, Lenin, Churchill, Hitler, Mussolini, Mao, Tito, Nehru, Castro and others in their historical context. A more important question than the first one is why and how do we know the individuals who we consider important in history? The answer to this question leads us to the historical sources and biographies and textbooks which make it possible for us to know these individuals in the first place. The need to know these important individuals is political. The social use of their memory is therefore political. It is useless to say that plain curiosity leads a reader or observer to the story of an individual because that curiosity itself is located in a political context. Why are we curious about some and not others? In order to fully comprehend the character of an important individual in history we must go to the texts which have created and re-created him or her for our times. This is important because far too often our view of our heroes and villains is coloured by bestsellers, hagiographies and media reports. Whether we uncover hitherto unknown truths about the past associated with these leaders is not the point. The point is to understand the textual process through which the individual comes to be imagined in our cultural consciousness. All this, of course, does not suggest that the obvious need be doubted. Who can doubt that Hitler was responsible for the Holocaust or Churchill was responsible for the Bengal Famine of 1943 or Stalin was responsible for the decimation of the Bolshevik old guard. Knowing an individual means going beyond these obvious documented truths. It means understanding the historical context within which an individual can be placed meaningfully. Towards this end this chapter presents a short commentary on Shivaji Maharaj, a medieval Maratha ruler loved and revered by modern

Indians as a champion against Aurangzeb's unjust policies in the 17th century.

In many societies the contested social memorialization of men, more so great men, is often caused by the ideological mixture of folklore and historiography. In the case of the 'great' men and women of the modern era usually plenty of documentary evidence exists for scholars to reach their conclusions. The collected works of many leaders are available to everyone. Books written by these men like the ones on the Second World War by Churchill and the history of India by Nehru remain popular. But this is not the case with medieval or ancient individuals. In their case we must depend on court chronicles, commissioned histories wherever possible, travellers' accounts and other traces. In societies where printing did not develop and a great of knowledge remained oral, folklore produced the initial stories of individuals upon which later work was constructed. Often folk tales originated and evolved in historical periods which were not contemporaneous with their subjects. In the case of many kings and queens, myths entered their histories from poetry or cinema. The mythical queens Padmavati and Jodha Bai are two such cases. In Indian history men immortalized by a combination of anecdotes and chronicles abound; Buddha, Ashoka, Prithviraj Chauhan, Rana Pratap, Akbar, Aurangzeb, Shivaji, and many others. The certainty with which we can speak of Vivekananda, Gandhi, Jinnah and Nehru is absent in our dealing with pre-modern men and women. It is a different matter that the memory of even these men, like the subject of history itself, is never a settled matter across time and space. Modern media can reveal, hide or distort truths at will. Much passes on WhatsApp in the name of history these days. Take the contentious image of Aurangzeb, for example. We have no all India survey of the 18th century which can tell us what Indians thought of him. There is also no survey of the early 19th century which reveals popular opinion of the late Emperor. We also do not know whether ordinary Muslims, say in Kerala or Bengal, were sympathetic to his policies. We do not know whether Aurangzeb was a true representative of South Asian Muslims in general. Many important Marathi sources of the 18th century do not refer to Aurangzeb at all. If the tyranny of Aurangzeb was not remembered in much of the 18th century why and how did it become an important historical issue in the 19th century? That is the question. In Aurangzeb's case, the die was cast for the Western educated Indian when Elphinstone's pioneering authoritative observations labelled him "a sincere and bigoted Mussalman"[3]. This accusation became a permanent feature of most descriptions of Aurangzeb since the 19th century and, via Jadunath Sarkar's tomes, became the common sense about the maligned Emperor at least among the educated. By the early 20th century the name of Aurangzeb was associated with 'Islamic' tyranny the trope of which colored the growing communal consciousness of people living under British rule. By translation and pamphleteering the stories of his tyranny spread among those educated in the vernacular. The textbooks were complicit in the project. However, research on his reign continued and many critics of the villain were puzzled when Athar Ali's statistical masterpiece conclusively proved that the court of this 'bigot' had more Hindu nobles than the court of the tolerant Akbar[4]. If Aurangzeb hated Hindus, why was that so? Why did the Rajputs and other non-Muslims serve him with professional dedication? Further, the record of conversions during his reign does not lend weight to what the critics have said for a long time. In recent times the story of the enigmatic Aurangzeb has been thoroughly revised by Audrey Truschke who asserts that the "suggestions that the Rajputs and Marathas who resisted Mughal rule thought of themselves as 'Hindus' defying 'Muslim' tyranny are just that: modern."[5] Even the hagiographic account of Haldighati by Kesari Singh, a master of *Dingal* and English, highlights facts which inveigh against interpreting Rana Pratap's resistance to Akbar as an instance of Hindu resistance to Muslim domination[6]. It seems the terms 'Hindu' and 'Muslim' themselves meant something different from their modern connotations in medieval India[7]. Recent scholarship suggests that many terms we use to identify ourselves, in all probability, came into widespread social use because of colonial policies and knowledge in the 19th century. The well-researched submission of the late Edward Said that the orient was constructed by the Eurocentric ideological project of modern Western colonialism obviously has some merit. Thus the image of Aurangzeb was created, recreated and politically used first by the British and later the Indian nationalists and communalists to serve their interests. The British wanted Indians to believe that British rule had liberated them from medieval (read Islamic) darkness, whereas the communalists wanted to convince their followers that this darkness was a consequence of 'Islamic' rule over the subcontinent for eight hundred years. We find the fusion of colonial and communal perspectives in the imagination of Aurangzeb as the archetype Muslim tyrant. The story of Shivaji was also constructed simultaneously as a binary heroic counter-narrative to the debunking of Aurangzeb. For how can you have a villain without a hero and vice versa?

The memory of Shivaji has filtered down to us through several interpretative layers. Beginning with his eulogy by the contemporary poet Bhushan and the *Sabhasad Bakhar* (1694) written not long after his death (1680), for three hundred years Shivaji has been memorialized and canonized by his admirers. He lives in the *powadas*, *bakhars*, histories, cinema, television and social media dedicated to his greatness in modern India and especially Maharashtra, a linguistic state created in independent India. Shivaji is inseparable from the identity of a modern Maharashtrian. So central is Shivaji to Indian feelings about nationhood that it can be said that the history of a modern Indian identity which started in the 19th century is incomplete without reference to him. The nationalist historians and the political activities of Bal Gangadhar Tilak whose hundredth death anniversary falls in 2020 constructed the Shivaji of our historical imagination. Shivaji thus emerged as a symbol of a resurgent Indian nation in the 19th century. And yet Shivaji's memory remains besieged by the differing ideas of being Indian. His claimants and their ideological intentions are mentioned in the terse, articulate and immensely popular *Who Was Shivaji* by the late Govind Pansare[8]. Broadly speaking, the narratives about

Shivaji fall into two categories. The first has been popularized by the essentially Brahminical ideologues of Hindutva according to whom Shivaji was a *Gau Brahman Pratipalak* (custodian of cows and Brahmins) dedicated to upholding the social hegemony of *savarna* Hindus threatened by Muslim tyranny. According to the Hindu nationalists *Hindavi Swaraj* or *Maharashtra Dharma* meant the rise of anti-Muslim nationalism in the Deccan in the 17th century. Therefore, Shivaji's war against Aurangzeb was no less than a war of national liberation waged by a people united under his charismatic leadership! This claim has been made despite the terms *Hindavi Swaraj* or *Maharashtra Dharma* not abounding in the sources. Shivaji claimed descent from the Rajput Sisodias of Mewar, was crowned in accordance with prescribed *shastric* rites by Gaga Bhatt and his *Ashtapradhan* (advisory council of eight ministers) were mainly Brahmins. This is true but it is questionable whether becoming or aspiring to become an ideal Hindu Raja in medieval India can be squared with an ideology which emerged in the 19th century under colonialist ideological influence. The Brahmins comprised the literati in medieval Deccan and were employed regularly by both Muslim and Hindu rulers. It seems Shivaji continued this policy. If the employment of Brahmins is taken to mean the establishment of a Hindu Swaraj we might have to extend the argument to the Muslim Sultans of the Deccan as well. To take another example. Most of the Nizam *Deshmukhs* and *Deshpandes* were Marathas and *Deshast* Brahmins. From this should we deduce the nature of the Asaf Jahi state?

The second view projects Shivaji as an ideal *secular* king dedicated to the welfare of his subjects most of whom were the *shudra* peasants. Jyotiba Phule, drawing upon folk memory and inspired by the work of Shivaji, wrote a *powada* describing Shivaji as a *kunbi-kshatriya kulbhusan* who fought simultaneously against the Brahman and Yavana oppressors in Maharashtra[9]. Almost hundred years later Govind Pansare expanded the perspective on Shivaji by suggesting that the Raja's popularity be ascribed to his pro-subaltern political steps taken against the feudal *jagirdari* ruling class of medieval Maharashtra comprising the *saranjam* and *watan* holders. In the words of the slain Communist, Shivaji "turned the commoners into great people. They, in turn, made him a great king. Both came together to fulfil a tremendous task."[10] It is said that the teachings of the roving Bhakti saint-poets of Maharashtra and their love of the vernacular deeply affected the lives of the masses and set the cultural context for the rise of a Maratha power heralded by Shivaji. This argument was also presented by M.G. Ranade at the turn of the century in *The Rise of Maratha Power* (1900)

That Shivaji was exceptionally considerate towards the *rayats* and checked the power of the entrenched *watandar* class is underlined by the didactic *Ajnapatra* (1715) written by Ramachandra Pant *Amatya*, a surviving Brahman of Shivaji's advisory council. The *Ajnapatra* emphasizes that a sovereign, following Shivaji's example, should never expropriate anything, including dead trees embodying the labor of the poor, from the people by force[11]. By all accounts, Shivaji was, or at least perceived himself to be, a just ruler in accordance with medieval conventions. Evidence also suggests that he had no "rooted hatred of the Mahomedans" as Grant Duff claimed in the first 'modern' history of the Marathas written from a colonialist perspective[12]. While everyone believes that Shivaji was an ideal ruler, what remains unclear in public history is his relationship with Islam and Muslims. In this respect some facts, which must be repeated now, tell an interesting story. Recounted below is his relationship with Muslims which is hidden from public memory in the time of pretentious social media history. Some Maharashtrian Brahmans have claimed Shivaji because after all the Peshwai which replaced Shivaji's *swaraj* in the early 18th century had the blessings of Shivaji's grandson Shahu. *Kunbi* peasants, most of the latter day Marathas, and even medieval police castes like the Ramoshis have also staked their claim to Shivaji's memory[13]. English officer-ethnographers in the early 19th century discovered and documented the subaltern popularity of Shivaji decades before the nationalists wrote of him as a 17th century champion of a Hindu nation. But contemporary India must examine the possibility of the Muslims, especially the Marathi or *Dakhni*-speaking Muslims, partaking of Shivaji's political legacy.

The military connection of the *Verul*-based Bhonsale clan with the Deccan Sultanates is well documented. Shivaji's immediate ancestors were high ranking military commanders of the Adil Shahi and Nizamshahi Sultanates and had cultivated long standing cultural connections with the Deccan Sufi *pirs* and their *dargahs*. While the role of Malik Ambar and the Ahmadnagar regime in the military and economic rise of the Marathas is well known, the *syncretic* religious beliefs of the Maratha clans of the period must be remembered to the public. Shivaji's grandfather Maloji (1552-1606), a deeply religious man, was a disciple of both Shaikh Muhammad and Mahadeva[14]. Maloji named his sons Shahaji (1599-1664) and Sharfiji (1596-1624). They were born after he received the blessings of the Muslim Sufi saint Shah Sharif. The tradition of remaining a lifelong pupil of a Sufi *pir* was followed by Shivaji despite the spiritual influence on him of Ramadas Samartha during his last few troubled years (1672-80). Among his known saint-gurus was Baba Yakut of Kelsi whose shrine received regular grants from the royal treasury[15]. Like most rulers in medieval India, Shivaji made no distinction between Hindu and Muslim saints honouring them equally. We are told that he erected a "special mosque" in Raigad, his capital, for the Muslim devotees among his subjects alongside the Jagadishwar temple in which he prayed every day[16]. Even the outer architecture of this Raigad temple contains features of a mosque in line with the syncretic Deccan architecture of the period. From a distance this famous temple looks like a mosque with its central elongated dome and minarets. Tourist guides in Raigad accept that once upon a time a mosque too existed in Raigad but no mosque has survived the vagaries of time. In fact, my trip to Bijapur, Janjira and Raigad in March, 2020 just before the Covid 19 lockdown took me to various tombs in the region and I could not help notice the architectural similarities between the Adil Shahi Ibrahim Rauza, the royal tombs of the Sidis on the Janjira coast and the Jagdishwar temple in Raigad. These similarities suggest the prevalence of continuities between the Deccan Sultanates, the Siddis of Janjira and Shivaji's regime.

Many of Shivaji's trusted naval admirals like Daulat Khan, Siddi Misri and Ibrahim Khan were devout Muslims and even the servant who covered his escape from Agra at the cost of his own life was Madari Mehtar, a Muslim *farrash*. Obviously his life post-1666 cannot be imagined without this iconic escape made possible by a Muslim's self-sacrifice. More Muslim commanders like Siddi Hilal and Noor Khan Beg are mentioned in the sources. It is also known that the practice of enlisting Pathan soldiers in the Maratha armies goes back to 1648 when, on Gomaji Naik's advice, Shivaji employed five to seven thousand Pathans who came over to Shivaji from Bijapaur. In view of these well documented facts of Shivaji's life and work, the nationalist historian Sardesai was right in saying that, "Shivaji was in no way actuated by any hatred towards the Muslims as a sect or towards their religion. Full religious liberty for all was his ideal and the practice in his state."[17] While those alive enjoyed the liberty of worship and security of service even slain political enemies, like Afzal Khan, were buried with honour. Shivaji never dishonoured the Koran or a Masjid during his military operations across the Deccan. One aspect of Shivaji's resistance to Aurangzeb's invasion of the Deccan and economic impositions must be mentioned to underscore his nuanced understanding of Mughal rule in India. In a letter to Aurangzeb protesting the imposition of *jazia,* Shivaji heaped praise on Emperor Akbar calling him a *Jagatguru*. He wrote glowingly of Jahangir and Shah Jahan, praising them for following in the footsteps of Akbar and "never" resorting to "injustice." In his carefully chosen words these Emperors preceding Aurangzeb "had always their eyes fixed on people's welfare." According to Shivaji, by departing from the fair policies of his predecessors towards all their subjects, Aurangzeb was setting an example of bad governance[18]. In this letter Shivaji did not conflate either Alamgir or his ancestors with Islam per se; for a ruler, in his view, all subjects Hindu, Muslim or others were equal and deserving of consideration. Therefore, *Jazia* had to be opposed despite large sections of the Hindu elite being exempt from it. After all its weight would fall disproportionately on the poor which included the lower castes, the *Janata Raja* understood.

The historian Cynthia Talbot has asserted that historical memories survive in society in the layers of descriptions produced by the bards and historians over centuries[19]. In her re-telling of the story of Prithiviraj Chauhan she reveals the polyphonic nature of the sources which narrate the life story of an interesting historical figure. The dominant image of Prithiviraj is enmeshed with the mythology of Chand Bardai and the historiography of Hindu nationalism but there are other sources which speak differently of him. These, including the Jain accounts, should also be studied by the scholar to arrive at a more balanced assessment of the Chauhan King's character. In any case the latest layer of historical memory is always the contemporary layer produced by the overt politicization of history. These layers of memory contain important individuals as sites at which historical and ideological collective memories converge to buttress contemporary social identities. The historian must show why and how this memory is produced stage by stage and whether there are indeed multiple memories of a fetishized subject. If multiple memories of a historical subject exist, it is our duty as historians to understand and explain why one of them over time becomes dominant to the extent of erasing the others? Thus the *Samrats*, *Rajas*, *Sultans* and *Badshahs* of Indian history are remembered as good, bad, benevolent, great, patriotic, bigoted, foolish, treacherous, etc. The tendency of authors to write hagiographies of their favorite historical heroes in defense of their political positions adds more layers to the available historical memory in society besides promoting the history of elites. Consequently, these historical actors continue to excite differing, adulatory and critical passions among their detractors and appropriators. The active involvement of the public and market in such elite centred polemical debates sidelines other, and more meaningful, kinds of histories. In Maratha historiography and public history two names emerged as major sites of collective memory in the second half of the 19th century; Shivaji and Panipat.

The third site, Bhima-Koregaon emerged as a symbol of Dalit political assertiveness in the 20th century thanks to Ambedkar and his followers. It is tempting to apply Talbot's model of historical layering to these names and sites. Like Prithiviraj Chauhan, both subjects Shivaji and Panipat are intertwined with Hindu nationalism in the contemporary popular imagination saturated by social media images. Their Bollywood and media versions are the latest layers constructed by the establishment friendly filmmakers as the historical 'truth'. The mob is swayed. But these images are superimposed over other images and must be peeled off to perceive what lies beneath them. While celebrating Shivaji's birthday every year we must re-interrogate his story present in the layers of memory which began their journey into our lives from the 17th century itself. Upon revisiting the Shivaji of our times we might answer whether he belonged equally to his Muslim, Hindu and other subjects. If he did, even the non-Hindus have a legitimate claim on his memory. He invited an Englishman to witness his coronation ceremony and this representative of the Company has left behind a fair description of the occasion. During his raids on Surat he left the Company unmolested. He seems to have been particularly considerate towards the *sowkars*, meaning traders and shopkeepers, who brought capital into his domains and this model of promoting trade and thereby taxable money appears in the *Ajnapatra*. These facts increase the number of claimants to his memory.

Whether the masses of India living beyond the Western Deccan in the 17th century had heard of his exploits is a different and difficult question to answer in the context of medieval India.

NOTES

1. G.S. Sardesai, *New History of the Marathas Volume 1*. Mumbai: Phoenix Publications, 1946, p. 250.
2. *Who Was Shivaji (Shivaji Kon Hota?)*. New Delhi: Leftword Books, 2015, p. 55.
3. Mountstuart Elphinstone, *Aurangzeb*. New Delhi: OUP, 2008, p. 7 (first published in 1841).

4. M. Athar Ali, *The Mughal Nobility Under Aurangzeb*. Delhi: OUP, 1966.
5. *Aurangzeb: The Man and the Myth*. Gurgaon: Penguin Random House India, 2017, p. 82.
6. *The Hero of Haldighati*. Jodhpur: Books Treasure, 1996.
7. For more on this see Richard King, *Orientalism and the Myth of Modern Hinduism*. New Delhi: Critical Quest, 2008.
8. *Who Was Shivaji (Shivaji Kon Hota?)*.
9. The Shivaji of Mahatma Jotirao Phule, Full Text Marathi Powada on Shivray.com
10. *Who Was Shivaji (Shivaji Kon Hota?)*, p. 17.
11. *Ajnapatra* (edited by P.N. Joshi). Pune: Venus Prakashan, 1997, p. 48; The word used is *balatkar*, the Hindi Marathi word for rape.
12. *History of the Mahrattas*. Bombay: Cooper and Co., 1878, 4th Edition, London: Times of India Office, p. 107.
13. On the Ramoshi claims see Captain Alexander Mackintosh, *An Account of the Origins and Present Condition of The Tribe of Ramoossies Including the Life of the Chief Omiah Naik*. Bombay: American Mission Press, 1833.
14. A.R. Kulkarni, *The Marathas*. Pune: Diamond Publications, 2008, p. 7.
15. Sardesai, ibid., p. 269.
16. Ibid., p. 265.
17. Ibid., p. 269.
18. This letter is quoted by Sardesai and Pansare although in the latter's English version of *Who Was Shivaji* the date of the letter is 1657. Either Pansare got the date wrong or the publishers made a mistake. The *jazia*, with several exemptions, was imposed by Aurangzeb in 1679 in violation of Mughal practice since Akbar's times.
19. *The Last Hindu Emperor Prithiviraj Chauhan and the Indian Past 1200-2000*. New Delhi: CUP, 2017.

Select Bibliography

A.R. Kulkarni, *The Marathas* (Pune: Diamond Publications, 2008).

Al-Biruni, *India* (New Delhi: NBT, 1993).

Alun Munslow, *Deconstructing History* (London: Routledge, 1997, Special Indian Edition, 2007).

Anirudh Deshpande, *Class Power and Consciousness in Indian Cinema and Television* (Delhi: Primus Books, 2009).

Arthur Koestler in Richard H. Crossman (ed.), *The God that Failed* (New York: Columbia University Press, 2001).

Arthur Marwick (ed.), *Total War and Social Change* (London: Macmillan, 1988).

C. Wright Mills, *The Sociological Imagination* (London, New York: OUP, 2000).

Captain Alexander Mackintosh, *An Account of the Origin and Present Condition of the Tribe of Ramoshis Including the Life of the Chief Oomiah Naik* (Bombay: American Mission Press, 1833).

Cynthia Talbot, *The Last Hindu Emperor Prithiviraj Chauhan and the Indian Past 1200-2000* (Cambridge: CUP, 2017).

Donald A. Ritchie, *Doing Oral History–A Practical Guide* (Oxford: OUP, 2003).

Dorothy M. Fugeira, *Aryans, Jews, Brahmins: Theorizing Authority Through Myths of Identity* (New Delhi: Navayana, 2015).

Dr. B.R. Ambedkar, *The Untouchables* (Delhi: Siddharth Books, 2008 [First Published 1948]).

Eileen Ka-May Cheng, *Historiography: An Introductory Guide* (London: Continuum, 2012).

Eric Berkowitz, *Sex and Punishment–4000 Years of Judging Desire* (London: The Westbourne Press, 2013).

G.S. Sardesai, *New History of the Marathas Volume 1* (Bombay: Phoenix Publications, 1946).

Govind Pansare, *Who Was Shivaji (Shivaji Kon Hota?),* (New Delhi: Leftword Books, 2015).

Grant Duff, *History of the Mahrattas* (Bombay, Cooper and Co., 1878, 4th Edition, London [First Published 1827]).

Hayden White, *Metahistory: The Historical Imagination in Nineteenth Century Europe* (Maryland: John Hopkins University Press, 1973).

Jan Vansina, *Oral Tradition As History* (Madison, Wisconsin: University of Wisconsin Press, 1985).

John Tosh, *The Pursuit of History*, Sixth Edition (London: Routledge, 2015).

Karen Armstrong, *Islam: A Short History* (London: Phoenix, 2006).

Karen Armstrong, *Muhammad–Prophet for Our Time* (London: Harper Press, 2006).

Keith Jenkins, *At the Limits of History: Essays on Theory and Practice* (London: Routledge, 2009).

Kesari Singh, *The Hero of Haldighati* (Jodhpur: Books Treasure, 1996).

Kiran Nagarkar, *Cuckold* (New Delhi: HarperCollins, 1997).

Laura Mulvey, Visual Pleasure and Narrative Cinema, *Screen* 16.3 Autumn (1975).

Leopold von Ranke, *Selected Works Volume 3: From Vormärz to Prussian Dominance, 1815-1866*, Excerpts from *Selected Works (1824-1881)* [German History in Documents and Images online].

M. Athar Ali, *The Mughal Nobility Under Aurangzeb* (New Delhi: OUP, 1966).

Marc Bloch, *The Historian's Craft* (New York, Vintage Books, 1953, Indian Edition, Delhi: Aakar Books, 2017).

Marcia Landy, *The Historical Film: History and Memory in Media*, (London: The Athlone Press, 2001).

Marnie Hughes-Warrington, *Fifty Key Thinkers on History*, Third Edition (London: Routledge, 2015).

Michael Gottlob (ed.), *Historical Thinking in India* (New Delhi: Oxford University Press, 2006).

Mountstuart Elphinstone, *Aurangzeb* (New Delhi: OUP, 2008, first published 1841).

Natalie Zemon Davis, *Fiction in the Archives: Pardon Tales and Their Tellers in Sixteenth Century France* (Stanford: Stanford University Press, 1987).

P.N. Joshi (ed.), *Ajnapatra* (Pune: Venus Prakashan, 1997).

P.N. Joshi (ed.), *The Shivaji of Mahatma Jotirao Phule*, Full Text Marathi Powada on Shivray.com.

Partha Chatterjee and Anjan Ghosh (eds.), *History and the Present* (Ranikhet: Permanent Black, 2002).

Patrick Finney, 'Hayden White and the Tragedy of International History', www.allacademic.com (San Francisco: International Studies Association, March 29, 2008).

Paul H. Clyde and Burton F. Beers, *A History of Western Impacts and Eastern Responses, 1830-1975–The Far East*, Sixth Edition (New Delhi: Prentice Hall of India Private Limited, 1976).

Paul Sutermeister, 'Hayden White, History as Narrative: A Constructive Approach to Historiography', December 2004, Scholarly Essay, GRIN Verlag fur akademische Texte, http/www.grin.com (Geneva: Graduate Institute of International Studies, 2005).

Paul Thompson, *The Voice of the Past* (Oxford: Oxford University Press, 1988).

Perez Zagorin, 'History, the Referent and Narrative; Reflections on Postmodernism Now', *History and Theory*, 38, 1, 1999.

Peter Burke, *The French Historical Revolution: The Annales School 1929-89* (Stanford: Stanford University Press, 1990)

Philip Gourevitch, *We Wish to Inform You That Tomorrow We Will Be Killed With Our Families–Stories from Rwanda* (New York: Picador, 1998).

Prachi Deshpande, *Creative Pasts: Historical Memory and Identity in Western India 1700-1960* (New Delhi: Permanent Black, 2007).

Raziuddin Aquil and Partha Chatterjee (eds.), *History in the Vernacular* (Ranikhet: Permanent Black, 2008).

Richard King, *Orientalism and the Myth of Modern Hinduism* (New Delhi: Critical Quest, 2008).

Robert Brent Toplin, 'The Historian and Film: Challenges Ahead', *American Historical Association, Perspectives* (April, 1996).

Robert Perks and Alistair Thomson, *The Oral History Reader* (London: Routledge, 1998).

Romila Thapar, *The Past as Present: Forging Contemporary Identities Through History* (New Delhi: Aleph, 2014).

Ruth Balint, 'Where are the Historians?', *Inside Story*, July 30, 2009 [http://inside.org.au/where are the historians/inside story].

Shahid Amin, *Event, Metaphor, Memory: Chauri Chaura 1922-1992* (New Delhi: Penguin, 2006).

Simon Gunn and Lucy Faire (eds.), *Research Methods for History* (Edinburgh: Edinburgh University Press, 2012).

Sumit Sarkar, *Writing Social History* (Delhi: Oxford University Press, 1998).

Thomas Lee Charlton, Lois E. Meyer and Rebecca Sharpless, *Handbook of Oral History* (New York: Altamira Press, 2006).

Umesh Bagade, *Ambedkar's Historical Method* (New Delhi: Critical Quest, 2015).

Willie Thompson, *Postmodernism and History* (New York: Palgrave Macmillan, 2004).

Yves Thoraval, *The Cinemas of India* (Macmillan, 2000).